WALKING HOME

FROM EDEN TO EMMAUS

MARGARET GUENTHER

Morehouse Publishing
NEW YORK · HARRISBURG · DENVER

WALKING HOME

FROM EDEN TO EMMAUS

MARGARET
GUENTHER

Unless otherwise noted, the Scripture quotations contained herein are from the New Revised Standard Version Bible, copyright © 1989 by the Division of Christian Education of the National Council of Churches of Christ in the U.S.A. Used by permission. All rights reserved.

Morehouse Publishing, 4775 Linglestown Road, Harrisburg, PA 17112

Morehouse Publishing, 445 Fifth Avenue, New York, NY 10016

Morehouse Publishing is an imprint of Church Publishing Incorporated. www.churchpublishing.org

Cover design by Christina Moore
Cover art courtesy of Thinkstock

Library of Congress Cataloging-in-Publication Data

Guenther, Margaret, 1930-
Walking home : from Eden to Emmaus / Margaret B. Guenther.
    p. cm.
ISBN 978-0-8192-2395-1 (pbk.)
1. Walking in the Bible—Meditations. 2. Spiritual life—Biblical teaching.
I. Title.
BS680.W15G84 2011
242--dc22
                        2010044759

Printed in the United States of America

Table Of Contents

❦

Introduction

❦

Where Have I Come From, and Where Am I Going?

To begin with a confession, shameful in our motorized society: I have never learned to drive. Despite at least three attempts to learn and even the acquisition of a valid driver's license—how I passed the road test remains a mystery—I remain distinctly out of step in our high-speed world. Now, perhaps not always honestly, I can plead age and diminishment. I could well be a menace on the interstate or even in the Safeway parking lot. Over the years I have traveled happily by plane, ship, train, subway, bus, and by hitching rides with kindly people who are going my way.

But my favorite mode of travel is putting one foot in front of the other. Sometimes marching purposefully with a goal in sight, but also trudging, meandering, running, occasionally skipping, plodding, or dragging my feet and risking mishap as I look back at where I have been. An inveterate walker, I like to experience my world up close. I love to walk on the dirt road in Jenkins Hollow, in late summer watching the butterflies congregate around a perpetually damp spot where an underground spring threatens to break through. There is so much to see—a small bug I might have passed by unnoticed, amazing variations of color in the mosses that grow in wet places on the roadside, fascinating evidence of the animals who passed through before me, the bears, foxes, and raccoons who leave their calling cards in their distinctive scat.

I love to walk in strange cities, enjoying the adventure of getting lost while at the same time knowing I am quite safe. A few years ago in Beijing, the staff at my hotel catering almost exclusively to foreigners kept urging me to travel by cab as I set out to explore the city where I knew not one word of the language and could not read the street signs. I was adamant, however, so we finally compromised with a card to be carried with me everywhere: "This person is a guest at the Imperial Hotel." In other words, "If you find this demented woman wandering around and obviously lost, put her in a cab and send her back to us."

When I moved to New York over thirty years ago, it stunned me to hear certain streets described as beautiful. I don't mean elegant Park Avenue before it turns into Harlem or the pricy shops on Madison Avenue. My native New York friends meant "ordinary" streets in slightly rundown neighborhoods. In the streets where I walked daily, at first I could see only the detritus of their careless inhabitants—trash of all sorts, the occasional lost or abandoned garment or shoe or even underwear. (How, I asked myself, did that happen?) The absence of grass and exuberant trees depressed me. The city trees, if there were any, planted along the curb looked more like prisoners than flourishing examples of God's handiwork. The yardless houses, jammed together, and the apartment buildings, whether elegant or shabby, were no part of nature but rather reflected the harsh reality of an ungracious, crowded-together world.

But over time my vision improved and I was able to see things I had passed over. Perhaps a window box overflowing with petunias and geraniums, or a lovely architectural detail on an otherwise crumbling brownstone. Perhaps in springtime an extraordinary luxuriant wisteria that somehow managed to thrive in a most unlikely environment. (In twenty years I never figured out why wisteria vines seem to love their harsh environment.) Even the ailanthus, Tree of Heaven, despised by farmers and nature lovers in my beloved Blue Ridge Mountains, managed to thrive in the midst of pavement and polluted air. Nor will I ever forget my delight when I discovered a shabby little store that sold only glass animal eyes, useful only to taxidermists. It was just a few steps from a generic fast food restaurant and a shop that specialized in saris.

So over the years I have found myself ruminating on the wonder of walking. I remember squinting through a microscope in freshman biology, staring at tiny one-celled creatures, seeking evidence of their motility, which is what distinguishes us animals from plants. Moreover, our upright posture as bipeds distinguishes us from all the other mammals except from our cousins the other primates, whose posture is almost but not quite as elegant as ours. I shall never forget the day when my youngest child, whose boon companion on the floor had been the family dachshund, suddenly stood up for the first time and towered over his canine friend. Until then, I hadn't realized that a dog could look surprised. My infant son had made a statement of his humanity, to the astonishment of his doggy buddy, and their relationship was unalterably changed.

Somewhere, lost in a lifetime's accumulation of crumbling paper, is my birth certificate. It's on black paper with the relevant information in white ink—some primitive form of copying long before Xerox—and so old that it is beginning to tear along the creases. In the right lower corner of this precious document, promising that I am who I am, is the imprint of a tiny foot. In those days, this was proof of who I was at the moment of my entry into the world. I wonder if the person who rolled my brand new foot in ink had any notion of how many miles that foot would cover.

Our reflex to keep those two feet moving is inborn. I have read but never dared test this premise on my own infants or on the borrowed babies of others: if you hold the tiny creature by its arms and dangle it over an empty space, the little feet, suspended in mid-air, will make a stepping motion. If this is not true, it should be. We are born to keep moving.

The idea for this book came from a retreat that I offered several years ago with the title, supplied by the group that invited me, "A Closer Walk with the Lord." At first the idea seemed sentimental, even trite, but as I worked with it, I found myself even more aware that we are always on the way, that we are never at home, never "there" until the second great threshold is crossed. Old-fashioned German obituaries never spoke of a person's dying or "passing away." Instead the notice would read, "So-and-so has gone home—*ist heimgegangen*." The point of all our walking (tedious or joyous, rambling or purposeful) is going home.

So this book is a series of reflections about different "walking stories" in Scripture, beginning with the expulsion from Eden. Except for his triumphal entry into Jerusalem, mounted on a donkey, Jesus walked everywhere with his disciples. He was always arriving, on the way to somewhere else, or departing. The disciples were sent out with practically nothing, but for their walk they were permitted a staff and sandals. Not quite barefoot, but their feet must have been a mess—gnarled, scarred, and filthy. Adam and Eve walked out of the garden, Abraham and Isaac walked up to Mt. Moriah, the Israelites walked for forty years through the desert, the Prodigal Son walked home barefoot, and the disciples encountered the risen Christ as they walked to Emmaus.

Traveling the road can be tough. If we walk the walk, our feet will get dirty, worn, and blistered. Boots and shoes, sandals and sneakers, can protect and shield us. But the walk demands that we stand on solid ground, that we feel the earth beneath our feet, like Adam and Eve, when we go barefoot from the garden, ready to start a lifetime of walking.

Chapter 1

You Can't
Go Home Again

Then the Lord God said, "See, the man has become like one of us, knowing good and evil; and now, he might reach out his hand and take also from the tree of life, and eat, and live forever"—therefore the Lord God sent him forth from the garden of Eden, to till the ground from which he was taken. He drove out the man; and at the east of the garden of Eden he placed the cherubim, and a sword flaming and turning to guard the way to the tree of life. (Genesis 3:21–24)

I've never been thrown out of anywhere, yet. I'm well behaved in church, department stores, concerts, and rarely frequent bars. I can't even imagine getting kicked out of Eden: I'm too much of a conformist to break the rules. But then, who knows? That smooth-talking serpent might have convinced me that I wouldn't get caught, and no big deal if I were.

This may be blasphemous, but I am also convinced that life in the Garden of Eden lacked excitement. Perfection can become too predictable. If I remember correctly from a reluctant and compulsory reading of *Paradise Lost* long ago, Adam was puttering around doing something not particularly interesting or necessary—just killing time—while Eve tended the roses and came up with her theory about the division of labor:

❧

> *Let us us divide our labours, thou where choice*
> *Leads thee, or where most needs, whether to wind*
> *The Woodbine round this Arbour, or direct*
> *The clasping Ivie where to climb.* (IX. 214–217)

❧

But while there was plenty to do, what with naming and tending to the animals, and trying to curb the "wanton growth" of paradise with Eve's secateurs, there was no danger. All the creatures, vertebrate and invertebrate, were presumably friendly; even the snake was not venomous, just sneaky. He was not yet slithering around on his belly and hiding in the grass, hissing out seductive words. There was clean water and plenty of vegetarian, or more likely vegan, fare: theirs was the perfect Mediterranean diet now touted by our nutritional gurus. No need to do the laundry since they hadn't discovered the need for clothing, and the weather was no doubt mild. So how did the troublemaker get in, or at least get their attention? How did *curiositas* become an avenue to sin?

Little kids get into trouble when they are bored. All the toys in the world plus unlimited high-sugar snacks aren't enough. Why play with your big, brightly colored blocks when you can stick a finger into a live socket? Or fall down the stairs while exploring the world and testing your new-found but unreliable mobility? Or simply satisfying your curiosity, enchanted by the prospect that each new discovery would lead inexorably to a new and dangerous challenge?

As far as I know, we have the thirteenth-century theologian Thomas Aquinas to blame for identifying curiosity as a sin, the insatiable itch that killed the cat. The wanting to know perhaps more than we should, more than is good for us, more than we need to know. I still recall one of my mother's most irritating statements whenever confronted by mystery: "Well, we just aren't meant to know." But why plant that irresistible tree in the center of the garden and then caution this absurdly naive pair: "Whatever you do, don't go near it!" Was the God who designed paradise capable of an oversight? Or poor judgment of character? Or just carried away with his creativity? And why pick on the snake? Serpents are, after all, beautiful and fascinating. Crows are natural troublemakers, and cats are not trustworthy. Why not add a crafty and inventive snake to liven up the critter population?

God's reaction to their disobedience reminds me of the parenting style of Bronson Alcott, who clearly thought that he was God or at least a good nineteenth-century imitation. As a character-building exercise, he would put a delicious, shiny red apple on the table, then leave one of his four daughters alone to be tested. When Louisa, ever the adventurous one, succumbed and took a bite, she had to confess, repent, and grovel in her sinfulness. Bronson, like the God of Eden, wasn't into corporal punishment; that would have been too easy. Temporarily expelled from the austere Eden of her father's approval, Louisa no doubt got the message: that juicy, irresistible fruit is dangerous! Don't even think about touching it!

My earliest coherent memories go back to when I was about two and a half years old, three at the most. I had memorized the Lord's Prayer and said it every night along with "Now I lay me." The word "temptation" fascinated me, even though I had no idea what it might mean. Its syncopated rhythm had a jaunty, bouncy sound, and anything with four syllables was a treasure to be added to my growing vocabulary. But the meaning of the word was quite beyond me: it never occurred to me to lust after anything beyond willing grownups to read to me, a garden—not Eden, but still delightful—to play in, and a high-calorie dessert at six o'clock every evening. Even now, at the other end of life, interesting temptations have eluded or perhaps spared me. So when, in imagination, I join my sister Eve in the garden, I have to admire her intensity, her willingness to let go and risk all. Over the centuries artists have depicted a voluptuously beautiful Eve reaching for the apple. You could tell just to look at her that she was headed for trouble and taking the rest of us with her.

Scripture makes her "fall" sound easy: "So when the woman saw that the tree was good for food, and that it was a delight to the eyes, and that the tree was to be desired to make one wise, she took of its fruit and ate; and she also gave some to her husband, who was with her, and he ate" (Genesis 3:6). I have to wonder if it was really so simple. It might have taken days or weeks, months, even years before she took that final step. "Should I? Shouldn't I? Can I trust this charming, friendly serpent? His voice is so sweet—how could he be dangerous? I'll just walk a little closer to the tree and get a good look at the fruit again, smell its fragrance, admire its color. Maybe just a tiny bite? After all, God never told *me* that I couldn't have just one bite. He warned Adam before I was even around. Maybe he didn't mean me at all." Two steps forward and one step back. "Just a small bite. If it's really good, I'll go ahead and enjoy it. If Adam has some too, then it's not my fault. It'll be his problem then. Otherwise I'll hide the evidence, and God will never know."

Like the Alcott children, Adam and Eve first knew shame after eating the apple or pomegranate or whatever it was: they knew that they were naked. Experts in child development describe the stages of growing awareness as babies cease to delight in their nudity and first experience shame in their own naked bodies. I recall my own children scampering through the living room on their way upstairs to the nightly bath, shedding clothes along the way, and arriving in the bathroom ready to plunge into the tub. Eve and Adam were exposed in their humanity with no place to hide. They had lost their naiveté, their unblemished newness, their child-like ingenuousness. They were damaged goods. They were ashamed, although not of anything particular they had done—ashamed, simply, of their being. No wonder that they wanted to hide! Shame is so much more painful than guilt: it overwhelms. Whatever you have done to incur it, there is no way to undo it.

They are driven out, expelled. The gate clangs shut behind them, more final and drastic than changing the locks. That gate will not open again. There is no turning back: they can't go home again. There is a frightening, chilling finality about expulsion: there is no readmission, no second chance. All the pictures of the expulsion from Eden that I have seen and those that I have imagined have merged in my memory: the sun is not shining, Adam and Eve are cowering as they flee, an irate God looks down from heaven, and the cherubim are not to be messed with. This is the first hike alone, the first leave-taking, and it is filled with terror—the way is not clear, and there is no hope of homecoming. Did the God who sewed useful garments of animal skins think to make sandals or moccasins from the leftover scraps? Or are they driven into an inhospitable terrain with tender, vulnerable feet? After all, they hadn't needed shoes in Eden, with nothing dangerous to step on as they strolled around. But beyond the gate there must have been sharp stones, burning sand, mud, and treacherous ice. The author of Genesis doesn't tell us about that terrain. Was it a desert or a rain forest? Blistering hot or frigid? Filled with venomous snakes and mountain lions? Was poison ivy now twining around the roses? Scripture doesn't say anything about insects, so perhaps they were waiting just outside the gate for our human forebears to show up.

Whenever I ponder the shame, the fear, indeed the sheer terror of this story, I have to ask myself: was the expulsion necessary? Were Adam and Eve set up, or is that too harsh a word? Perhaps it was time for their next bold step. Growing up, accepting autonomy and maturity, means expulsion from paradise. Or maybe we outgrow paradise. Certainly it is a familiar phenomenon of human development that the child, then the adolescent, yearns to escape. Most earthly parents are less drastic or at least more subtle than the outraged creator God who tossed them out and barred the gate, but I am pretty sure that I would be tempted to change the locks if my middle-aged children wanted to move back in.

You can't go home again. These words became part of our consciousness, our intellectual and spiritual heritage in 1940, when Thomas Wolfe's final novel was published after his death. It may not be read much nowadays, but the words have stuck in our memory as a reminder what we don't live in Eden, that the gate is firmly shut and locked. They remind us that there is no going back. Home is not what or where we thought it was.

I think of the home of my childhood. Now and then, when I visit my town, I pass by the house where I grew up. It still stands on its quiet street, clearly loved and cared for by the current occupants. I want to go up on the porch, knock on the door, and hint that I would like to walk around the yard, maybe even manage a peek inside. But my cautious brother won't let me out of the car. He is right, of course. There is no going back.

Or I remember cities where I have loved and lived—Zurich, Cambridge, the upper west side of New York, even the Kansas town of college years. Physically, geographically they are still there, with some changes, of course, but still recognizable. But there is no going home, only the occasional visit. Home is seldom where we think it is. Perhaps we are always leaving Eden from the moment we emerge from our mother's body, the first day at kindergarten, through the storms of adolescence right down to the moment when we draw our last breath.

Chapter 2

Don't Look Back

Then the men said to Lot, "Have you anyone else here? Sons-in-law, sons, daughters, or anyone you have in the city—bring them out of the place. For we are about to destroy this place, because the outcry against its people has become great before the Lord, and the Lord has sent us to destroy it." So Lot went out and said to his sons-in-law, who were to marry his daughters, "Up, get out of this place; for the Lord is about to destroy the city." But he seemed to his sons-in-law to be jesting.

When morning dawned, the angels urged Lot, saying, "Get up, take your wife and your two daughters who are here, or else you will be consumed in the punishment of the city." But he lingered; so the men seized him and his wife and his two daughters by the hand, the Lord being merciful to him, and they brought him out and left him outside the city. . . . But Lot's wife, behind him, looked back, and she became a pillar of salt. (Genesis 19:12–16, 26)

One of my favorite pictures in the National Gallery, a holy place just a subway ride away, is Albrecht Durer's depiction of Lot and his daughters fleeing a devastated, stinking Sodom. It is a small painting on the reverse side of a panel depicting Mary and the infant Jesus. An interesting choice: on the one side, a tender depiction of maternal love, while on the other a family fleeing for its life. Lot leads the little procession, a prosperous-looking, pudgy German solid citizen. His well-dressed daughters follow at a respectful distance behind him, carrying substantial burdens. Mrs. Lot, with no name of her own, is barely discernable. Indeed you can miss her completely unless you know the story and know where to look: she is a tiny, blackened figure far in the background. No one else is on the path from destruction to safety.

Lot, unlike his uncle Abraham who is recognized as a prophet, is not to be taken seriously; a marginal note in my *Jewish Study Bible* refers to him as a buffoon. At the very least he is a thoroughly unlikeable and opportunistic man. Earlier, when it is clear that their large households and herds of livestock must part ways in the land of Canaan if they are to continue to prosper, his uncle offers him the first choice of new land, no doubt with the expectation that, according to tradition, his nephew would defer to his elder. Instead, Lot jumped at the chance to prosper and chose the fertile southeastern plains near the cities of Sodom and Gomorrah. The old man had been good to him, but after all it's only sensible to look out for number one.

To be self-serving is an unpleasant but recognizable human trait. But Lot as a family man is something else. Even as I try to persuade myself that different customs prevailed in other times and other places, and that hospitality especially was a sacred obligation, I cannot read the account of one terrible night in Sodom without a shudder of fear and rage. When the angelic messengers come to warn Lot of the coming catastrophe, he shelters them from the violence of the mob in the town square of Sodom. They batter his door and demand that the visitors be brought out to be raped as an act of humiliation. Lot, the good host, offers a compromise: "I beg you, my brothers, do not act so wickedly. Look, I have two daughters who have not known a man; let me bring them out to you, and do to them as you please; only do nothing to these men, for they have come under the shelter of my roof" (Genesis 19:6–8).

Were the young women—more likely, teenagers—huddled together in a corner, resigned and passive, or weeping and protesting? And were the divine visitors mere onlookers, or were they ready to explain to Lot that they could really take care of themselves, even destroy the angry mob on the spot, if he would just open the door and hand them over? As it turned out, the crisis was averted and the angels themselves had to protect their host before getting away unscathed the next morning.

But Lot still was negotiating his future. During his flight from Sodom, he dared argue with the Lord, who directed them to flee to the hills. "I don't want to go there," he countered, "it's too dangerous! I want to go to Zoar." So God changed the itinerary, and Lot's family walked to a nearby small town

We know nothing of his wife. Where was she when her daughters were at risk of being raped, and where was she throughout this whole puzzling story? If she had a voice, we do not hear it. If she feared her husband's anger, we do not know it. Was she weeping or silent? Embracing her daughters, trying to shelter them with her arms around them? Or was her spirit broken long ago so that she could not imagine disobeying or even mildly questioning Lot's wisdom? Was she gaunt and forbidding, or soft and warm? Maybe in her stoic uprightness she had begun already to be transformed into a pillar of salt.

I have to wonder why she chose to remain in such a terrible place, how she could disregard the divine command, "Flee for your life, do not look back or stop anywhere in the Plain; flee to the hills, or else you will be consumed" (9:17). One thing is clear: this divine imperative is not to be ignored. Yet it is only human to yield to the irresistible urge to look back. The unknown, even when it is desired or inevitable, can be frightening. There's an old Scots saying: Better the devil you know than the devil you don't. The Scot in me has an inkling of her inner debate: "Go? Stay? Maybe get a little way out of town and then look back to see how bad it is back there? I can always catch up with Father and the girls if it seems like a good idea. Especially if I don't drag a lot of furniture with me." After all, the known can offer a kind of security. One of the chilling moments from the film *Schindler's List* lingers in my memory: a patrician Jewish matron, being crowded with several dozen others into a small apartment, says, "At least we know it won't get worse than this."

And, of course, Lot's wife may have paused and looked back out of curiosity; it is not every day that you can see sulfurous fire raining on your city. She might have looked back with regret: everything that she had cherished in her household was destroyed. The good china, the girls' baby pictures, even the pots and pans. Or with pleasure: those terrible people of Sodom are finally getting what they deserve. Or fatigue: I'm not able to start all over in a new place. Rotten as it was, this place was home. Or her reaction might have been simply a matter of temperament; some of us are never quite ready to take the next step into the unknown.

And why was she so strangely and so harshly punished? Scripture isn't helpful here. Commentators offer the explanation that she is still there on the outskirts of the vanished Sodom, a human-like formation of salt testifying to the truth of this story. Jesus was the first to suggest that she was being punished as, describing the chaos and catastrophe of the last days, he warns his hearers not to look back: "On that day, anyone on the housetop who has belongings in the house must not come down to take them away; and likewise anyone in the field must not turn back. Remember Lot's wife" (Luke 17:31).

And why salt, treated so ambiguously throughout Scripture? We are the salt of the earth, Jesus tells us, yet salt is also symbolic of sterility and unfruitfulness: salting of that same fertile earth by the conqueror could be a final blow of devastation to a defeated people. Yet through the centuries salt has been a valuable, indeed precious commodity all over the world. Moreover, salt is part of our humanity. Our bodies contain salt, our sweat and our tears are salty, and we need it even when the Morton's is banished from our own kitchens for the good of our blood pressure. Should God one day choose to turn *me* into a five-foot-one-inch pillar, he would first need to augment my chemical makeup with a divinely supplied addition of sodium chloride.

Lot's wife refused to take the first step of the walk and, even worse, she looked back. Some women are nesters, and at various times in my life I have numbered among them. I have never gone, even on a freely chosen and much desired move, without looking back, without hesitating if only for a moment before I closed the door on the old dwelling for the final time. From my crowded dorm room as an undergraduate to my most recent move from a house down the street to a manageable apartment, and all the places in between, I haven't been able to resist casting one last look back. Were I to find myself in prison someday—wrongly convicted, of course—I would have a rueful moment when the warden came to tell me that I was free to go. After all, I had learned what to expect. As one of my friends who has experienced life inside would say, I could count on "three hots and cot." Not much fun, but predictable. Who knows what might be lurking just outside the door or around the corner?

So life in Sodom couldn't have been easy, but after all it was home. And as for that command to flee: couldn't there be time for one last look around? Lot and the girls had fled carrying big bundles, but only a good housewife can recognize the essentials. Surely the omnipotent God could hold off the rain of fire and sulfur for another thirty minutes!

Lot's wife, I think, is a negative example of how to close the door on the past with a sigh of mingled regret and relief, and get walking. There must have been many reasons why she chose to remain in a dead, uninhabitable place that was no longer home. I wish that she had been able to trust the promises of that fierce God who loves us and promises to save us. Then, with or without a hastily assembled parcel of odds and ends, she could have taken that first step and not merely watched her girls recede into the distance, balancing their bundles on their heads. Did she want to call out to them? Did she admire their obedience, their sense of adventure?

This is one of the stories where I want to argue with God, "You have gifted us with memory. Not only can we not help looking back, we learn from it and even grow." Our deepest and true stories are based on reflection on the path we have already followed. Otherwise, why is the youngest child at the Seder enjoined to ask, "Why is this night different from any other night?" Now there is a ritual, a script for this solemn celebration; but I can imagine that in the early days the old folk leaned back in their chairs, maybe topped off the wine glasses, and started telling the story, maybe interrupting each other with additions and corrections. And the child who set it all off with a truly urgent question, learned where he had come from and who he was from those stories.

Pictures of my parents and grandparents look down on me from the top shelf of my computer desk. My father looks very much as I remember him: gentle, benevolent, and wise, with just a hint of a mischievous twinkle in his eyes. My German grandparents are upright, stoic, no-nonsense folk; I suspect that the ordeal of being photographed frightened and oppressed them. My mother looks a lot like me, with her head tilted slightly to the side; my close friends tell me it is my own look when I am paying attention. My grandmother, whom I knew only as an old woman, is beautiful and my Scottish grandfather, whom I knew only as a very old bald man, is a gorgeous blond. As they look back at me wordlessly, they remind me where I have come from, they remind me that I am part of the long family walk that my children and grandchildren will continue when I have gone far enough. They remind me to keep looking back as I continue to look forward, a feat that my ophthalmologist would judge impossible if I tried to accomplish it literally.

Surely there is a lesson here. There are different ways of looking back. Like the child at the Seder, we can yearn to know who we are and where are our roots. When we look back on our own little lives, if we can manage such retrospection honestly, we can rejoice in what we have been given. We can trace the path winding away behind us and chart the bumps in the road, the times when darkness fell before we had reached the day's stopping place, the times when we ploughed through snowdrifts, the times when we fell either painfully or with a total loss of dignity on the ice. We can see all the places where we took a wrong turn, all the places where we received generous and unexpected hospitality. We can see how the walk strengthened us even if, when we reached the end, we were worn out and quite ready to cross the second great threshold. We can see ourselves clearly, maybe for the first time.

Chapter 3

The God
Who Hears

When the water in the skin was gone, she cast the child under one of the bushes. Then she went and sat down opposite him a good way off, about the distance of a bowshot; for she said, "Do not let me look on the death of the child." And as she sat opposite him, she lifted up her voice and wept. And God heard the voice of the boy; and the angel of God called to Hagar from heaven, and said to her, "What troubles you, Hagar? Do not be afraid; for God has heard the voice of the boy where he is. Come, lift up the boy and hold him fast with your hand, for I will make a great nation of him." Then God opened her eyes, and she saw a well of water. She went, and filled the skin with water, and gave the boy a drink. (Genesis 21:15–19)

I have great affection for Hagar. I am moved by the poignancy of her story and love her for her refusal to knuckle under and accept unfairness and maltreatment at the hands of those who owned her. After all, she did behave provocatively, indeed cruelly, to Sarah. With Sarah's approval, even encouragement, Abraham "went in" to Hagar, and when she saw that she had conceived, Scripture tells us, then Hagar treated her mistress with contempt. A gentler, more deferential woman would have known her place and enjoyed her triumph over her mistress in secret. But all in all, she is a strong, attractive figure, even if quite uppity, and I am proud to claim her as sister and ancestor.

I've ruffled a couple of feathers in the parish where I serve when I offer my own version of a blessing from one of our supplemental liturgies and speak of "the God of Sarah and Hagar and Abraham." The rector hasn't said anything, but one of our more formidable matrons demanded, "Who is this Hagar, anyway? You're always adding extra women to everything!"

Who is this Hagar, anyway? Where does she fit in our great family album of the faith? What is distinctive about her walk, her flight as a fugitive, and then her cruel casting out to almost certain death, these are walks not chosen, but taken out of desperation and helplessness. "Hagar the Egyptian," as she is called, is the other, the outsider, the foreigner in Abraham's household. She is the truly inconsequential, unacceptable one. She owns nothing. In the eyes of her envious mistress she is merely a rival and a fertile body. But she is also a tough woman.

This is a troubling story in which everybody is wrong and everybody might be a little bit right as well. Sarah is suffering the shame and disgrace of barrenness—unexplained and unmerited, but accepted by all as the will of God—and her solution, although repellent to us, was acceptable in her society. Sarah has behaved according to the law. Abraham too is behaving according to the accepted moral code when he simply steps out of the conflict and returns Hagar to her slave status and whatever mistreatment Sarah might visit upon her. Now that he has sired a son, he might well turn his back on the emotional and spiritual conflict in his household: "Leave me out of it. You take care of it."

Hagar's first walk is really blind flight from Sarah's vengefulness. Scripture doesn't give us details. Abraham has said to his wife, "Your slave girl is in your power; do to her as you please." And Sarah "dealt harshly with her" (Genesis 16:6), which could mean anything from the assignment of impossible tasks, deprivation of food and rest, or physical and verbal punishment. Whatever form it took, whether subtle or cruel, Sarah's "harshness" made life unbearable. Unlike the children of Israel, Hagar has no Moses to harass Pharaoh, to negotiate deadlines, and to organize her departure. She's on her own, running blindly, impulsively. There is no evidence that she kissed her baby (now Sarah's) good-bye or that she gathered or stole a few provisions for her flight. Unlike Mary on the flight into Egypt, she is without support, without a plan, and with no hope of return.

The real heart of the story, the part for us to chew on, lies in two questions, posed to her by the "angel of the Lord" who finds her by a spring in the wilderness on the way to Shur. This is no Christmas card angel, easily recognizable by his big wings and flowing locks, nor the kind of New Age angel we can find in the self-realization section of bookstores, but the stern angel of the Hebrew scriptures, God's messenger, who is simultaneously challenging and comforting. There is nearly always considerable holy confusion and merging in these stories of the encounter with the divine messenger. Is this a heavenly emissary or just a prescient passerby asking the questions that need to be asked? Or is it God? Or, as we sometimes find on multiple choice tests, all of the above?

This angel asks the important questions: "Hagar, slave girl of Sarah, where have you come from and where are you going?" Like so many of us, maybe most of us, Hagar knows where she has come from, but can't begin to address the second question. She is fleeing in desperation, running away but not running toward.

God's messenger might well have said, "There's good news and bad news." What he did say was, "Return to your mistress and submit to her," and surely Hagar's heart must have sunk at the command. But it must have leapt at the accompanying promise: "I will so greatly multiply your offspring that they cannot be counted." And there is the even greater promise, and I am convinced that this is the important one: "The Lord has given heed to your affliction." Good news and bad news. Defeat and victory. All in the same package.

Hagar knows what has happened to her: she has encountered God, the God who hears. Perhaps outwardly nothing has changed—indeed she is even worse off than before because she must return to slavery and Sarah's anger. But at least for the time being she knows where she is going, to whom she truly belongs. Her first walk has been a false start. The walk with God or toward God must have a purpose beyond escape from the harshness of life. The Israelites of the Exodus knew that they were moving away from exile and slavery and toward the freedom of the promised land. Hagar knew no such thing.

Her story seems like a foreshadowing of the courage and desperation of the slaves of our own national past. The Underground Railroad offered respite and help on the dangerous trek to freedom, but historians tell us that the fugitives also relied on a sign in the heavens: the North Star, the Big Dipper, or as they called it, "The Drinking Gourd." That sign in the night sky carried the promise of water, refreshment, and restoration along the way. But for Hagar there were no guides to lead her to the next station, no promise of water in the desert, no signs along the way. The angel of the Lord is a tough one—I'm not sure that I would derive much comfort from his command to turn around and go back. I would have liked a little kindness, some recognition that my child had been stolen and that I was desolate. Hagar returns to the only home she knows. Does Abraham even look at her? Is Sarah generous enough to find her useful? Could she look at her son and know that he was no longer her son?

After the birth of Isaac there comes fresh trouble and a time for the next walk, the next departure from the known into the unknown. Hagar's son Ishmael has been displaced by the real heir, and he is big enough to be a troublemaker. They are expelled, kicked out: "So Abraham rose early in the morning, and took bread and a skin of water, and gave it to Hagar, putting it on her shoulder, along with the child, and sent her away. And she departed, and wandered about in the wilderness of Beer-sheba" (Genesis 21:14). These are meager supplies, just enough to get mother and child out of sight and out of mind. They are really being sent away to die, although no one, not even the author of Genesis, is so crass as to mention it.

Now the water and the bread are gone. She is indeed ready to die. As the first sign of maternal tenderness—or is it possibly hardness of heart—Hagar realizes she cannot watch her child die, so she moves away from Ishmael, "about the distance of a bowshot," sits on the ground, and weeps aloud. And this is where the story ends. God's angel speaks to her from heaven and says to her, "'What troubles you, Hagar? Do not be afraid; for God has heard the voice of the boy where he is. Come, lift up the boy and hold him fast with your hand, for I will make a great nation of him.' Then God opened her eyes, and she saw a well of water. She went, and filled the skin with water, and gave the boy a drink" (Genesis 21:17–19).

That is the end of the story for Hagar. She has been merely a vessel, a container. Ishmael is the child of promise, who has been saved for greatness. But I am convinced that she is among us still, that hers is more than an ancient story of harshness and desperation. In some ways, her story is still being played out, although perhaps not as crushingly as the story teller of Genesis presents it.

I wish I knew the next steps of Hagar's walk. Did she hunker down by the miraculous well to live out her days? Did she somehow make it back to Egypt? Did she curse God and his servant Abraham who used her and then cast her aside? What was the rest of her walk like, and where did it end? Could she find it in her heart to know that the Lord God had walked with her?

Chapter 4

Are We There Yet?

> *So the two of them walked on together. Isaac said to his father Abraham, "Father!" And he said, "Here I am, my son." He said, "The fire and the wood are here, but where is the lamb for a burnt-offering?" Abraham said, "God himself will provide the lamb for a burnt-offering, my son." So the two of them walked on together.* (Genesis 22:7–8)

I remember walking with my children when they were very young, steady on their feet, but with short legs that couldn't move very fast and got tired easily. It was sheer pleasure when we had no urgent errands or appointment times looming; otherwise it could be exasperating. When I was in a hurry to get where we were headed, the walk could be joyless and laborious for all of us.

Walking with children has its own special flavor. Maybe because they are closer to the ground and see things that even the most observant tall person might miss, such as caterpillars, moss, muddy puddles, dead leaves, and decaying, fascinating trash. Maybe because the world is still new to them, creation's minutiae are not minutiae at all. Or possibly because they didn't want to go on the walk in the first place, at least not on a walk programmed by an all-powerful adult with specific goals and an inexorable time table in mind. They dawdle, or they run ahead when cautioned to stay close.

Children want to be picked up and carried when they are perfectly capable of walking. They refuse to hold a hand. They like to throw rocks into streams and ponds. They explore not only with their hands and eyes, but with their mouths—all the detritus that gets picked up, tasted, licked, and chewed. And always attractive is the prospect of wading noisily through deep puddles. The purposeful march is not for them!

In Scripture one of the most poignant stories of a parent walking with a much loved, cherished child is the account of Abraham and Isaac leaving Sarah at home and setting off with two servants, a donkey, and a load of wood split by Abraham himself. We know that Abraham had a finely honed knife with him, but probably he kept that hidden. The mother in me identifies with Sarah; surely she had questions about this unexpected outing. "Where are you going? Will you be home for supper if not for lunch? Have you water? Something warm to wrap up in if you are gone all night? Look out for the boy— he's still very young, and he's never been away from me before. In fact, I'm not sure this is a good idea at all!"

I always picture a sunny morning, late spring or maybe early summer. Sarah is busy: there is washing to be done, food to be cooked, and the servants to be supervised or harassed, depending on her mood. Hagar is the chief irritant and always has been. Sarah doesn't like the way Abraham stares at her when he thinks she isn't looking. So in some ways it's probably a relief when Abraham announces that he and the boy are going away for a few days, one of those father-son bonding experiences that will be good for the child, make a man of him. And no lunch to prepare and no dinner to think about, a mini-holiday for her and an outing for the men.

Isaac was probably pleased to have his father's total attention. Did he jump up and down at the idea of an unexpected camping trip with his father? Did he pelt him with questions, just to receive the same reply: "You'll see. Tell your mother goodbye, and let's get going."

At the beginning of the trek he behaved about like my own young son, squatting down to examine plants and insects, scrutinizing a mystery hole or crevice in the rocks where a snake might live, wandering off the path to study a fascinating weed, watching the clouds move across the sky, trying to act as tough and grown-up as the two servants.

It turned out that they wouldn't be home for lunch or even for supper. That was never the plan. I suspect that the adventure had pretty well worn off by the third day. In my imagination I hear bits of conversation. "Are we there yet?" repeated perhaps every thirty minutes. That plaintive question would quickly give way to others. "My feet have blisters. . . . The bug bites itch. . . . I'm tired. . . . Carry me. . . . I want my mother. . . . I'm hungry. . . . I'm thirsty. . . . The sun is too hot. . . . It's no fun sleeping outdoors. . . . I want to go home." Anyone who has walked with a small, increasingly unwilling child can augment this litany of questions, complaints, and protests.

And what about Abraham? Was he paying attention to what should have been their last conversation, or was he preoccupied, sad? Isaac was his treasure, the yearned-for son who had come to him as a gift from God. Did he think about dumping the load of wood, turning around, and heading toward home? Or did he cajole and command his son to "straighten up"? Maybe he promised a big surprise at the end of the trek, and they passed the time singing the first-century equivalent of "Ninety-Nine Bottles of Beer on the Wall" or "The Wheels on the Bus Go Round and Round." In exasperation Abraham must have said more than once, "Stop whining. You're a big boy now."

The story turns dark by the third day. What did Isaac think when his father dismissed the servants and loaded down his son with the wood for the sacrifice? It had to be a sizeable bundle to build a fire big enough to consume a young boy. No more playing along the way, wandering off the path, or chasing butterflies. He's figured out that this is serious business, that some young animal will be ritually sacrificed. And where is that animal?

Did Isaac submit to the binding, being tied down with ropes, with trust or terror? Was his faith in his father so great that he was able to persuade himself that this was just some sort of a game that Abraham was playing? Or was his father angry? Punishing him for some offence of which he knew nothing? Testing him? What was it like to lie there helpless, looking at the sky while his father, whom he trusted, loomed over him with a large, sharp knife? Did he scream and struggle, repeat his cries to go home to his mother?

Nor does the author of Genesis tell us about the trip back down the mountain, after God intervened and provided the sacrificial ram caught fast in the thicket. Did Isaac skip ahead with joy at having been saved? Or had he lost all trust in his father? What did he say to Sarah at the homecoming? "It was okay. I missed you. I got tired. Nothing much happened."

I think about this story when people tell me that the Bible is the great source book of family values. Wouldn't Isaac's experience of his trusting walk up the mountain turn him into someone incapable of trust ever again? Wouldn't it drive an irreparable wedge between Abraham and Sarah, defying the skill of the wisest marriage counselors, even Dr. Phil or Oprah? What kind of God, I wonder, would demand such a sacrifice, even if he planned this last-minute rescue? What kind of God would subject a human family, no doubt doing its fallible best, to such a cruel test?

The mother in me wants to rewrite the story from Sarah's viewpoint. Had God deigned to speak to her and command, "Take your son, your only son Isaac, whom you love, trek up the mountain, and offer him as a burnt offering," I'm willing to bet that she would have replied, "No way! That's one walk we're not going to take."

Chapter 5

Take Off Your Shoes

When the Lord saw that he had turned aside to see, God called to him out of the bush, "Moses, Moses!" And he said, "Here I am." Then he said, "Come no closer! Remove the sandals from your feet, for the place on which you are standing is holy ground." He said further, "I am the God of your father, the God of Abraham, the God of Isaac, and the God of Jacob." And Moses hid his face, for he was afraid to look at God. (Exodus 3:4–6)

It must have been an ordinary day. Moses might well have been quite content with a simple and uneventful life tending the sheep of his father-in-law, Jethro. He might well have been grateful, whether by accident or divine providence, just to be alive. His life story up to now has read like a cliff-hanger. As the child of an enslaved Israelite in Egypt, by royal edict Moses should have been killed at birth, but thanks to his resourceful mother and intrepid sister, he grew up in the royal household as the adopted child of Pharaoh's daughter. Now he's a fugitive, a murderer, albeit for a just cause and with exemplary motives— he has murdered an Egyptian for beating a Hebrew kinsman, covered up the evidence, and fled. Moses, never considered by himself or others as a leader, is now completely dependent on his father-in-law for shelter and safety. At this point, he does not seem a likely candidate to do God's work in any big way.

So there he is, in the middle of nowhere, surrounded by somebody else's goats or sheep. I have never tended a flock, but I have to imagine that it would be tedious work, long stretches of time with nothing happening, nothing very interesting to look at, at least not until nightfall when the stars came out. My only comparable experience was decades ago, when as a teenager I was recruited by my father to catch up on months of neglected filing. So there I was, in a hot corner of a large office, looking out on a grubby alley, and confronted by piles of paper as tall as I. This was of course in the pre-electronic age when such dreary stacks proliferated almost by magic, to be put neatly in order in gray metal cabinets and never looked at again. It's the only job I ever hated. Each day was the same, never punctuated by any experience remotely interesting. Even watching sheep and goats mill around in the alley would have been more interesting.

The angel of God appeared to him in a flame of fire out of a bush. We know that it was a divine visitation because the writer tells us so, but Moses just saw a bush on fire. Intentionally set afire or spontaneous combustion? Or maybe his eyes were playing tricks in the bright sunlight? Or was the bush far enough off the path to need a second look? So Moses looked, and the bush was blazing, yet it was not consumed. Was it a big bush? A little bush? It might have been just a tiny patch of dry, scruffy vegetation that could have ignited spontaneously, or a breath-taking, terrifying conflagration with flames and smoke reaching to the sky. Whatever it was, it aroused Moses' curiosity: "I must turn aside," he tells himself, "and look at this great sight, and see why the bush is not burned up."

Now God has got Moses' attention. He is willing to pick himself up, abandon his charges, and "turn aside" to draw closer to the mystery. Herdsmen, like bored young file clerks, have no agendas or plans beyond getting through the day, so diversions and distractions can be welcome. But Moses has seen something that he doesn't understand, something completely inexplicable. This can happen to anyone when, just at the edge of our peripheral vision, we glimpse something that astounds us, draws us closer, impels us to leave off what we are doing and to turn aside. I recall one summer afternoon in the Blue Ridge, when I wandered into the kitchen to put my coffee cup in the sink and just at the edge of my vision, barely perceptible but arresting, I glimpsed a sinuous black something under the kitchen table. As far as I know, it wasn't God, but a six-foot long black snake who had slipped into the house. I stopped short on my journey to the sink with the dirty coffee cup and paid attention.

Hoping that it would stay where it was and not slither off to a really good hiding place, I ran down the road to seek help from my retired bootlegger neighbor. He pinned it to the wall with a rake, while I lopped off its head with the pruning shears. It's the only creature I have ever killed, except for a wood rat that I shot with my BB gun in that same kitchen, and I wish now that I had been brave enough to scoop up my slithery friend and usher it out the door. There was room in this world for us both.

My black snake was hard to miss, but I have to ask myself how many burning bushes I have overlooked. How many times have I kept my eyes resolutely on the sheep and goats, persuading myself that the wisps of smoke and darts of flame were mere illusions or distractions? How many people—good, well-intentioned people—spend their whole lives as conscientious herdsmen and never notice a bush that is flaming away right under their noses?

When I recently reread this story, one I have known or thought I have known since childhood, I noticed a sentence that I had not seen before: "When the Lord saw that he had turned aside to see, God called to him out of the bush, 'Moses, Moses!'" It sounds as if God were as surprised as Moses. How long had that bush been burning in the arid solitude of the desert before anyone noticed it? How many herdsmen and travelers had passed by without a second glance? It is as if God were there lying in wait, hoping to be noticed. It is easy to forget that God is the God of surprises, an intrepid escape artist and master of disguise. Sometimes I am tempted to blame artists, especially Michelangelo, for giving us commanding pictures of the awesome creator God, never to be mistaken for an ordinary mortal and certainly not for a flaming bit of shrubbery.

So God calls Moses by name, and Moses gives the right answer, the only answer we *can* give when we hear God call our names. "Here I am."

To be called by name can be flattering—ah, I am special! I have been singled out for attention! Or alarming—why am I being paged, of all the hundreds of people in this busy airport? Perhaps I am being upgraded, or maybe the airport police have singled me out as the dangerous person I really am. Regardless of the circumstances, to hear our name called gets our attention. Even if we are ready to dismiss the burning bush as a curiosity, something one might find on the Discovery Channel, to be called by name unexpectedly is a surefire way of getting our attention. Even when the caller is a mere human, such as one of the distorted voices over an airport PA system or the counter person telling us that we can pick up our sandwich, our existence has been validated. We are known.

But here Moses hears the voice of God. This would be a good place for the story to end, both comforting and affirming. God and Moses have found each other. But as they say in those late-night television pitches for all-purpose kitchen gadgets— Wait! There's more!

It comes in the form of a caution, a warning: "Come no closer; take off your shoes, this is holy ground." It is a good reminder that we are called to approach the Holy unguarded, in all our human vulnerability. Those sandals protected Moses' feet from injury, from sharp stones, burning sand, scorpions, voracious insects. He could probably move faster, more easily when his feet were protected, but these useful sandals are a barrier now; they separate him from the earth that God created, keep him from remembering that he himself is only dust. The few naked steps off the path must remind him in his smallness of who he is.

Whenever I pass the majestic mosque in my city, I find myself wishing that we would emulate our Muslim neighbors who leave their shoes at the door. We can grow almost too comfortable and easy, almost casual in our relationship with the high-voltage God whom theologian Rudolf Otto termed "a tremendous and fascinating mystery." But then I, who am happiest and most comfortable, most fully at home when I can slip off my shoes, wiggle my toes, and feel the ground beneath my feet, must wonder. Is the command from the bush a reminder to put us in our place, or is it an invitation to feel at home, to come closer without fear?

God's message was one of compassion, challenge, and promise, all enmeshed and tangled together:

❦

> "The cry of the Israelites has now come to me; I have also seen how the Egyptians oppress them. So come, I will send you to Pharaoh to bring my people, the Israelites, out of Egypt." But Moses said to God, "Who am I that I should go to Pharaoh, and bring the Israelites out of Egypt?" He said, "I will be with you; and this shall be the sign for you that it is I who sent you: when you have brought the people out of Egypt, you shall worship God on this mountain" (Exodus 3:9–12).

❦

Yes, Moses' people are promised deliverance, they are promised abundance and safety, but Moses has to do the work. He must be the instrument. He must accept the terrible burden of partnership with the God who speaks from the bush.

Quite naturally, Moses feels inadequate: "Who am I that I should go to Pharaoh and bring the Israelites out of Egypt?" We know how the story ends. We have read the book and seen the movie, so we know that Moses accepts the job and agrees to take on this Mission Impossible. But not without a struggle— assigned by God to this dangerous, difficult task, Moses insists that he lacks eloquence. But God has no patience, with his excuses: "Get your brother Aaron to help you. He's a good talker. I'll tell you what to say, and you tell Pharaoh." Picture this fugitive shepherd, standing out in the middle of nowhere, arguing with a bush. When I am feeling brave, I try to put myself where his bare feet stood.

Moses must feel safer after God promises to be with him. But could he trust it? How would he know? Might there be other divine manifestations along the way that he could easily overlook? By now he would recognize any mysteriously burning bush along his path, but he must have suspected that God was unlikely to use the same attention-getting device more than once. Moses needs reassurance. So he asks, as I most certainly would be tempted to ask, "Who should I say is calling?" *I am Who I am* is not really a satisfactory answer, but it is all that Moses gets. God remains a mystery, to be approached with awe. Jesus gives us another name, *Abba,* and invites us to come closer. Both names are the right ones.

Most of the time I try to keep an eye out for burning bushes—on the Mall, in assorted airports, on Wisconsin

Avenue by Starbucks, in my own small study. Most of time I try to listen, just in case my name is called unexpectedly, and be ready to slip off my sandals or my grandmotherly sensible shoes or mud boots. Nothing must come between me and the holy ground. To the dismay of my Arkansas mother-in-law, who for several years sat in the corner rocker in my kitchen and watched me prepare dinner barefoot, I am happiest when nothing comes between my feet and God's sacred ground. Only naked feet can feel its holiness.

I learned this long ago in my childhood when, on a hot summer night, my father would say, "Let's take off our shoes and walk on the grass." Together we would walk down the four steps from the front porch onto the dewy lawn, look at the stars, and talk very softly. Or maybe say nothing, just enjoy the feel of the earth beneath our feet. None of the rose bushes burst into flame, and I never heard a voice inviting us to come closer. But, looking back, I'm sure that the great I AM was listening.

Chapter 6

The Way Out

At the third new moon after the Israelites had gone out of the land of Egypt, on that very day, they came into the wilderness of Sinai. They had journeyed from Rephidim, entered the wilderness of Sinai, and camped in the wilderness; Israel camped there in front of the mountain. Then Moses went up to God; the Lord called to him from the mountain, saying, "Thus you shall say to the house of Jacob, and tell the Israelites: You have seen what I did to the Egyptians, and how I bore you on eagles' wings and brought you to myself. Now therefore, if you obey my voice and keep my covenant, you shall be my treasured possession out of all the peoples. Indeed, the whole earth is mine, but you shall be for me a priestly kingdom and a holy nation." (Exodus 19:1–6)

T*he way out*. That is the literal meaning of "exodus," a word I learned long ago as a zealous and competitive little girl in the Roanoke Presbyterian Sunday School. In addition to memorizing acres of Bible verses—we all fell eagerly upon "Jesus wept" as a free pass to winning a minute gold star by our names on the chart—we were given the task of naming the books of the Bible in correct order. It wasn't official policy, but we preferred to rattle them off at breakneck speed, without pausing for breath. We had no clue what the names actually meant, but found Numbers easy and Deuteronomy a challenge. Exodus was at least short. This exercise served me well, decades later in seminary, when our Old Testament professor, appalled at the biblical illiteracy of the class, demanded that we at least get a handle on the raw material of the course. So I refreshed my memory and reeled off all thirty-nine names while most of my classmates struggled.

So that is all an exodus is: a way out. For the Israelites it was *the* exodus, the uncertain and laborious way out of slavery. It is a foundational story of our Jewish neighbors and, of course, foundational for us Christians as well. As the stuff of flamboyant movies of my childhood, it has taken me decades to separate out what I absorbed from the King James Bible and what I accepted as Holy Writ in the stuffy darkness of the neighborhood movie theater in Kansas City. Did Moses really look like Charlton Heston in that gaudy technicolor film with its casts of thousands, or was he an unprepossessing little man with a squeaky voice? After all, he tried to evade the divinely imposed call to leadership by assuring the Lord that his brother Aaron was a much better choice for the job.

Despite divine assurance that he was up to it, Moses wasn't much of a negotiator. Talk, threats, and a series of deadly plagues only hardened Pharaoh's heart. The only solution was a clandestine departure under cover of night. No time to pack, no time even to look at the place that had been a first, a welcome, then oppressive home for over four hundred years. Just prepare a special meal and then get going. I would have skipped the cooking and settled for whatever might be found in the kitchen, but the divine instructions are demanding, clear, and permit no improvisation. Cook it, eat it, dispose ritually of the remains, smear some blood around the door, and leave. There was no time to savor the poignancy of the last meal, the last hours in a familiar place. This meal must have been something like those times of sitting on the floor among packing boxes (no chairs—the movers have already taken them), the phone disconnected, sharing cold take-out pizza with my family. Home is no longer home. There is neither time nor purpose in looking back, and the future is too distant to be contemplated. These relatively comfortable, freely chosen circumstances must be a pale reflection of the Israelites' last hours in Egypt.

Surely there must have been at least one compulsive housewife who insisted on going back one more time to make sure that the stove was turned off and the door tightly locked. Surely there was at least one child who cried for a favorite toy that had to be left behind. Surely there was at least one aged person who protested, "I'm too old for this. Leave me here and let me die."

Would these despised slaves, despite the divine command, have embarked on the trek if they had had any idea of what lay ahead? I'm pretty sure that I would have tried to negotiate, at least asked for a map and a time table. And Moses' job of organizing this untidy group of walkers must have been horrific. The writer tells us that there were about six hundred thousand men on foot, not including women and children. The women didn't get counted, but I assume they were carrying whatever needed to be carried, including babies and children. (Women seem to do all the carrying, at least in the Bible.) After a few months, years, decades on the march it must have been a pitiable parade of the sick, the old, the dying, the variously impaired, the pregnant, the angry, the bereaved, and lots of little kids dragging their feet and demanding to go home. The very old must have forgotten why they embarked on the walk in the first place, and the sick must have prayed for death— "Don't worry about me. Just let me lie down by the path for a bit." The children grew up; the boys and girls figured out that hormonal urges don't go away even in the hardships of the desert trek. Their children had no idea what or where home was, if indeed it had ever existed. And I can't begin to imagine how many generations of sheep and goats lived and died before any of them reached the promised land.

This may be the first recorded adage that no good deed goes unpunished: Moses' leadership wasn't appreciated despite his ability to correct harsh circumstances with timely miracles. No water? Here it comes gushing from a rock. No food? Manna from heaven, which I suspect tasted a lot like unadorned tofu.

No doubt it was nutritious, but nothing like the tasty and healthful Mediterranean diet they had enjoyed in Egypt of fish, cucumbers, melons, leeks, and onions, all for free. Nevertheless Moses suffered from abysmal approval ratings, and behind the mistrust and the near rebellion there must have lurked the question: Is God to be trusted? This was a question too frightening to ask. Much better to grumble at Moses.

Slavery of all kinds can be seductive, if only because it makes life seem predictable. Life in Egypt had begun to look good, like the relative security and comfort of life in prison. It's not surprising that the Israelites looked back with regret when the novelty of their escape had worn off and fatigue, boredom, and disillusion set in. Egypt can look good when you are in the middle of the desert where all the landscape looks alike, the thrill of the pursuing chariots and parting sea has worn off, and there is no access to Mapquest.

I've never embarked on a real exodus, but I've wandered through several deserts, all too often failing to notice the pillars of cloud and fire that God sends before us to guide our way. Clouds can evanesce, just blow away as you come close to them. Or they can turn into rain. Or they can become thick fog that renders the path invisible. Clouds lack the solidity that inspires trust. And fire! From infancy we are cautioned: don't get too close to the fire. Keep your tiny hand off that hot burner! You can be badly burned, even killed. On my wanderings through woods and deserts, I much prefer neatly lettered signposts along the way, or at least the blazes on trees that mark the trails through our national parks.

Maybe I would notice the divine signs leading me on if I had a Moses as tour director. But then, like my Israelite forebears,

I'd probably stop trusting him quite early on the trek. Over the years, I have become convinced that, if we are spiritually alive, we keep repeating in our own small way the pattern of sanctuary, slavery, escape, and arrival in the promised land—and not just once but several times during a long lifetime. We don't notice upon arrival, when we set our bundles down and look forward to comfort and stability, that the land of milk and honey, if we hang around long enough, has a way of imperceptibly turning into Egypt.

My first exodus in late adolescence, when the home that had sheltered and nurtured me was turning into a benevolent prison, was a kind of mini-flight from Egypt. If I were to become a mature person, living into her gifts and responsible for her blunders, I had to hit the road. Too much of the same can keep us from growing up. If the Israelites trekked toward the promised land of milk and honey, I had to move out from a safe but circumscribed life. It was not quite flight by night, but it was far from easy. Like the Israelites, I thought I knew where I was going, but my path, like theirs, turned out to be a circuitous wandering. Along the way, life as a single-minded student, in love with earning for its own sake, was another welcoming Egypt that gradually became a mild form of slavery. The sumptuous feasts of academic life—more books than you can read, questions that lead to ever deeper questions, the companionship of like-minded seekers and mentors, the luxury of single-mindedness—are not unlike the cucumbers, leeks, and garlic that the fleeing Israelites looked back on with such yearning. Then, after more wandering, much of it through pleasant deserts, I was sure that I had arrived in Canaan. After all, what more could one want than a good husband, a doctorate in Germanic Languages and Literatures, a pleasant home, a fruitful lay ministry in a loving parish, and three quite adequate children? There was even a job that I loved, even if it didn't pay much; teaching hippies and eggheads at a local university was sheer joy. As in the Egypt of the children of Israel, the food was delicious and even the ongoing challenge of wearing three or four different hats and fitting thirty-six hours of work into twenty-four held few surprises.

So I was startled to find that my Canaan, my land of milk and honey, had bit by bit turned into Egypt. Even though I was making my modest quota of bricks with no oppressive overseers to harass me, it was time to hit the road again. The new Canaan turned out to be New York's upper west side, a richly rewarding, if dilapidated land of plenty. When I sought ordination to the priesthood, the old identity counted for nothing. My slate had been wiped clean; I was back to neophyte status. I still recall the day when one of the seminary professors returned a paper to me with the condescending but well-meaning words: "Margaret, you write very well." I wanted to kick him in the ankles and snarl, "Honey, I've been teaching people to write for twenty-five years." But instead I smiled meekly and said, "Thank you."

By then I had begun to figure out the pattern. Even with no Egyptians in sight, no cruel Pharaoh, and no omnipotent God speaking from the smoking mountain, I knew it would sooner or later be time to leave again. I'd also figured out after more than forty years of wandering, that I had to be my own Moses. I even began to envy the children of Israel a bit. They could always blame their God-appointed leader when the going got rough. They might be impatient when he vanished up the mountain for a consultation with the Almighty, but they must have realized the luxury that even an imperfect guide was better than none at all.

I'm pretty sure that I'm in Canaan now. But I've made the trip often enough to know that's there's no need to redecorate, even to unpack, because just when I get comfortable and even a tad complacent, it will be time to eat the farewell meal, put on my sandals, and depart in haste. I'm in no hurry. Happy to skip the ritual meal, I plan to close the door for the last time and start walking.

Chapter 7

Walking into Exile

By the rivers of Babylon—
there we sat down and there we wept
when we remembered Zion.
On the willows there
we hung up our harps.
For there our captors
asked us for songs,
and our tormentors asked for mirth, saying,
"Sing us one of the songs of Zion!"
(Psalm 137:1–3)

This is about the end of a long walk about which we have no cohesive narrative, but can visit only in our imagination. In 597 BCE the southern kingdom of Judah was conquered by the Chaldeans and the Judeans sent into exile in Babylon, including the aristocracy and the propertied classes. Only the poorest stayed behind. It is hard to find a coherent story of the nearly sixty years of exile, which runs like a thread through the history books of Kings and Chronicles and the oracles of Isaiah, Ezekiel, and Jeremiah. They did not return to their homeland for at least sixty years. The prophet Jeremiah, who remained behind in Jerusalem, insisted that the forced removal of the Judeans from their homes was a well-deserved divine punishment, and after they had served their time, they could come home. But of course, after so many years in an alien land, it would be a whole new group on the homeward walk.

Psalm 137 is the poignant lament of a captive people far from home, with no dream of returning. Their lament turns to fury by the end of these few verses, a curse aimed at their captors: "Happy shall he be who takes your little ones and dashes them against the rock!" Sometimes a psalm like this, with its mixture of anguish and fury, is what we need to hear, even when we yearn for soft words and pretty pictures. Sometimes we do need to feel far from home in a strange land, captive not in ancient Babylon, but captive nonetheless. The long walk is over and the walkers must make their home in a place that is no home. They don't belong there. Singing the old songs, especially under compulsion, won't help.

In some ways, the forced removal from Judah must not have been so bad as it might sound: only the more educated and useful people were forcibly removed after the defeat of their homeland. Over the decades of exile they learned to make themselves at home, and many became assimilated. New generations grew up who had no first-hand memory of the homeland, who knew it only from songs and stories. Much of the land they had left was redistributed, so the poor left behind were no doubt better off.

It is a long walk from Jerusalem to Babylon. No pleasant cities or probably not even many small villages along the way. Presumably these desirable, even valuable new captives were not driven cruelly by their conquerors, nor were they fleeing Pharaoh's chariots. But it was a long way. They had heard of Babylon, but they couldn't really know what awaited them. Scripture simply doesn't offer details. The triumphal return, many years later, is another story. Given the span of years, I can't imagine that many lived to experience this second walk. By then, a new generation had grown up.

When I am brave enough to let myself reflect deeply on my own history and what I think is a foreseeable future, I am reasonably certain that I am not about to be led into literal captivity in an alien land. Such a thing is unlikely in my pleasant corner of God's world. But not all the walks of the faithful people fall into the category of ease, civility, comfort, or the promise of a happy outcome. Exile happens when home is no longer home. When the walk is no longer a promising, challenging, maybe joyous adventure, but a walk into an alien land.

That definitive experience of leaving home with no hope of return, whether it be forced or voluntary, is unlike any other. My German forebears were not sent into exile in the mid-nineteenth century, even though there is a persistent family rumor that Grandfather Beltz was a draft dodger, eager to avoid conscription into Bismarck's army at all costs. But his poverty or restlessness led him to settle in a strange land, where he learned—not very well—a strange language and managed to survive. His was no exile like the captive Judeans, but I wonder how much he must have yearned for his own language? I know that he managed to sing the songs of his homeland because my father passed some of them on down to me. They were not heart-wrenching laments like the psalms, but simple little folk songs that would entertain restless children or pass the time when repetitive work grew tedious. His was no forced exile, but it helps me imagine that definitive departure from all that is familiar. There are still exiles in my own time, exiles that I know only second-hand, but join this bitter psalm in my imagination, for the history of the twentieth century was marked and scarred by exile.

The poet Dante, who knew from experience the pain and desolation of exile from his native Florence, wrote in *Paradiso*: "You will leave everything you love most: this is the arrow that the bow of exile shoots first. You will know how salty another's bread tastes, and how hard it is to ascend and descend another's stairs" (XVII: 55–60). It is the little things, the details, that count. I know that I am at home when I can walk through my house in the dark without bumping into anything, when I can comfortably walk up and down the stairs without looking. I know that I am home when the earth beneath my feet is solid. And to eat "another's bread"—it is not necessarily salty, but it just doesn't taste right. Maybe it doesn't even fit our definition of food.

A few years ago, leading a retreat in West Texas, I annoyed the cook when I repeatedly refused his enormous servings of rare beef. I was sure that it was a delicacy, but I just couldn't manage it and broke the local rules of hospitality. When living in Argentina, I carefully learned the words for local delicacies that I was sure would finish me off—*cesos* for brains, *pulpo* for octopus, *caracol* for snail. I was there in temporary exile so I never bothered to work out the fruits and vegetables, but animal proteins were another matter. And in my own part of the south, Virginia, I have never got the hang of grits or salt pork, perhaps the vanishing delicacy of another age. What were the Babylonian equivalents of unfamiliar or ritually forbidden foods? At what point did the exiles become hungry enough to break down and eat them?

But exile in our own time is more than enduring strange foods and finding one's way on unfamiliar terrain. Exile means that you are not at home. You are in a place where you do not want to be, leaving home without a change of address. More to the point, you are in a place where you are not wanted. Since I've never experienced literal displacement from my home, I can go there only in imagination. The squatters who populate my neighborhood Metro stop are exiled in a country where many are citizens. The frail aged are exiled, even when they are residents in comfortable "facilities"—the word "homes" is too ironic to be used in this context. There are those who have lost memory and speech, those who fill our prisons, those without hope, those who are shunned deliberately or unconsciously by those closest to them. Our world is filled with exiles. No need for them to walk hundreds or thousands of miles to an alien land.

How can they sing when they are so far from home? And where is home? And how do they find it again?

Chapter 8

Head for the Hills

In those days Mary set out and went with haste to a Judean town in the hill country, where she entered the house of Zechariah and greeted Elizabeth. When Elizabeth heard Mary's greeting, the child leapt in her womb. And Elizabeth was filled with the Holy Spirit and exclaimed with a loud cry, "Blessed are you among women, and blessed is the fruit of your womb. And why has this happened to me, that the mother of my Lord comes to me? For as soon as I heard the sound of your greeting, the child in my womb leapt for joy. And blessed is she who believed that there would be a fulfillment of what was spoken to her by the Lord."
(Luke 1: 39–45)

L uke doesn't say, but I always picture Mary alone when Gabriel comes to her and tells her not to be afraid. So many of these stories of divine intervention seem to take place on quite ordinary days, even on tedious, boring days. The scene has been a favorite of artists through the centuries, and usually Mary is seated in a sumptuous room, often with a book in her hand, surrounded by dazzling perspective, intricate architectural detail, and rich colors. She is young, beautiful, dressed in lavish, impractical garments, and her slender white hands look as if she has never done a day's housework in her life. The angel, beautifully androgynous with flowing locks, often carries a spectacular lily, which could almost be a weapon.

But a few years ago, when I was visiting a temporary exhibit of women's art in a small gallery, I came upon a refreshingly new take on the annunciation. I can't recall the artist's name, but I remember that she was from Nebraska, far away from a romanticized first-century Nazareth. I would love to find her and tell her that she gave me new eyes when I let myself live into this familiar story of my faith. The scene is a simple kitchen from the 1920s, without microwaves, marble-topped counters, or a giant refrigerator. Mary, a wholesome but far from elegant small-town midwestern girl, is seated at a plain wooden table, the kind that graced the kitchen of my childhood. Gabriel, with no lily and no flowing locks, very much resembles Henry

Kissinger in his prime. There is nothing soft or sentimental about this picture: it is a confrontation. Mary and Gabriel are leaning toward each other, almost lunging, arms outstretched, pointing at each other, not so much in hostility, but in intense encounter. They are clearly not whispering or speaking in loving tones—they are almost shouting at each other. They are both powerful figures, and it is clear that their meeting is not a casual one.

Mary is stunned. I can almost hear her say, "How did you get in? And what did you just say?" I can also picture her looking around for her mother, indeed for any ordinary person who might have been in the house that day. There is an electric connection between the ordinary girl at the table and God's powerful messenger, without anything heartwarming about it.

And this is no longer an ordinary day. Gabriel wastes no time in getting down to business: "Hail, O favored one, the Lord is with you." Who was he, and how did he get in? Luke tells us that Mary was troubled, even baffled, wondering what on earth was happening to her. So he comforts her a bit—"God's not angry at you. In fact, he's singled you out." Then he delivers his news: "Don't be afraid. But you're pregnant with a son who will be no ordinary child: indeed he will be the Son of God." At this point, I would ask him to repeat what he just said and then, like Mary, ask a very practical question: "How on earth can this happen? I'm not married. I'm a good girl, a virgin. What am I supposed to tell my parents? And what about Joseph?"

We need to watch out for holy messengers, not that we can avoid them if we are on their route on any given day. Sometimes our own annunciations feel like wonderful, happy news. The woman who has longed for a child experiences the first touch of morning sickness. Or the longed-for ideal job becomes a reality. Or the final chapter of the book is not only finished, but polished, if not to perfection then at least to something acceptable. But sometimes they are frightening, sheer bad and unexpected news rather than a promise of new life. A few cells in a biopsy, a devastating personal or professional loss both unexpected and undeserved, a sudden rupture in a neatly planned life. Sometimes they are merely puzzling: "Something has changed. What does it have to do with me? And what am I supposed to do about it?"

If I put myself in her place, I can only begin to imagine what Mary felt after this angelic intrusion into what must have begun as an ordinary day. Luke's story ends tersely, with one short sentence: "The angel departed from her." That was it. Not "I'll be with you every step of the way," or at least "I'll check in regularly." But instead Mary is left alone with an awesome, terrible, joyous secret. So she hastens to seek out a friend.

Mary's cousin Elizabeth, considered too old to bear children, is now six months pregnant. The angelic messenger hadn't spoken to her directly, but brought the good news to her husband Zechariah. Luke doesn't tell us much more about her, but I can picture her comfortably past the queasy first months and now quite enjoying her fruitfulness. As a cousinly friend, she's just the right person to share Mary's news: she knows about mystery, about surprises, and what it means to feel new life within her body. But she doesn't live next door. Not even in Mary's home town of Nazareth, but up in the hill country. So, Luke tells us, "She set out and went with haste into a Judean town in the hill country." This is no casual visit to a trusted friend and kinswoman. but an urgent mission. It is simply too much to sit alone with the terrifying message of the angel, wondering, "Is it good news or bad news?" Does it mean her disgrace and ruin, or exalt her to heights she can never imagine? If she were a teenager of today, her parents might probably be the last to find out what is going on in their daughter's life. How could she possibly explain what happened? And how could they believe this tall tale of an angelic visitation unless they were extraordinarily devout or gullible? And Joseph? I can't begin to imagine what courage it would have taken to initiate *that* conversation.

So Mary leaves home to seek out a trusted friend, old enough to have wisdom and experience but by no means parental. (Artists have depicted Elizabeth as positively ancient, but I suspect that she was still relatively youthful, at least by today's standards.) She is a mature woman, a trusted family member, but above all a friend. She won't scold—"You should have known better than to get in such a fix." Nor will she laugh at Mary's predicament and try to minimize it—"You think that *you* have troubles?" To visit an Elizabeth was and still is well worth the trip.

Mary "goes with haste" to see her friend. Scripture is full of these urgent departures. Here again, as I always do, I want Luke to fill in the details. Was it hard to get away from home? What did she tell her parents? Was it acceptable for a young girl to be traveling alone? Did she meet friendly, helpful people who walked part of the way with her, maybe shared food with her? Could she stop and rest for a bit under a tree? Get a drink of water from a well? Was she carrying a bundle of clothes and maybe a hostess gift for her cousin? Was the incline steep or gentle? You can get awfully tired, dizzy, and easily winded in the early days of pregnancy.

She didn't have to wait for symptoms; Gabriel had made it quite clear that she was expecting a child. But what did she know about pregnancy? And about birth? I remember long ago, when I was in graduate school, one of my friends was an older Jesuit who explained to me in a long conversation over coffee how Mary could have given birth without mess, blood, or loss of dignity. (I wish that I could fill him in on the details now!) Did Mary know what lay ahead, physically and emotionally? Elizabeth, older and wiser, might tell her the details even if she hadn't yet experienced childbirth herself. At any rate, to be left alone with her secret must have been unbearable. This is a walk unlike any other in Scripture: she is not fleeing from slavery, not leaving home like the Prodigal Son, nor has she been exiled from the comfort of her home, possibly in its own way a small paradise. She is on her own, maybe for the first time in her sheltered life, compelled to act out of her own strength.

The hill country was perhaps not a great distance in miles, and the road was well-traveled. Going to the hill country meant a walk to a different terrain—uphill most of the time, maybe steep, maybe gentle, but demanding strength and endurance. Mary must have felt very much alone, a little breathless, but filled with urgency. Her walk is neither flight nor escape, but rather a clarifying quest: not so much a physical as a spiritual distancing herself from what must have been inner turmoil.

This is a story about community, about spiritual friendship, about our loving support of one another. It is a story about our inextricable connection: for those who love one another, more importantly who love God and who would make a place for God within themselves. This is no ordinary friendship. Mary and Elizabeth are different in age, circumstances of life, and perhaps in how they felt about themselves. But they are bound together in their kinship, their friendship, and the fact that their worlds are being turned upside down. In my younger days we used the old euphemism for pregnancy—"She is expecting"—an expression that suggests hope, eagerness, a bit of anxiety. In old-fashioned German, it is even better: Mary and Elizabeth are of "good hope," *guter Hoffnung*. Elizabeth, past the age of childbearing, had thought that she was too old, that her life was essentially over. Now she finds herself on a wondrous threshold. And Mary is pregnant with God.

If this is a story of friendship, it is also a story of hospitality: When Mary arrives, Elizabeth is there waiting for her, putting herself aside to be wholly receptive. Her task is to listen, to be present, to discern, to speak a prophetic word. When I picture this story in my imagination, I see the two women sitting together companionably, comparing feelings and symptoms.

"I'm beginning to get some real backaches. I'll be glad when this baby is born! I'm too old for this—if God wanted me to have a child, he could have managed a miracle fifteen years ago."

"Food really tastes strange. Just about everything makes me sick."

"The morning sickness will go away in a couple of months. I'm not sure why on earth the creator God—blessed be his name—thought that we needed that along with everything else."

"When Zechariah first told me the story about the angel I was a little put out, but then I remembered that Sarah was the last to hear that she was pregnant. Why on earth can't God speak to us directly? But you got the word straight from the source."

"The angel was really sure that it will be a boy. I wonder how he knew. I hope he got it wrong because everybody says that girls are a lot easier. Boys can get into all kinds of trouble."

"You'll begin to show pretty soon. We'll need to make new clothes for you and the baby. And of course you can stay here as long as you want to. We never run out of things to talk about. Zechariah's work as a priest keeps him away, and he never was much of a talker anyway."

God chose to become incarnate and needed the hospitality of a woman's body to accomplish this. The fourteenth-century Dominican mystic, Meister Eckhart, would say we all await the birth of God in the soul. What happens in this story is not a matter of sexuality or anatomy because we can all be pregnant with God, carry the spark of Christ within us. And like Mary, we cannot go it alone. The joy of all new life must be shared. As Mary, we need our Elizabeths. Like Elizabeth, we need to be welcoming presences. The roles can be reversed—many times if we live long enough and are willing to leave home to head for the hill country.

Rarely can these encounters with the Spirit be planned. Mary hadn't called Elizabeth for an appointment because she knew she would be welcomed. The Elizabeths of the world don't always have an electronic day planner to organize their days or even old-fashioned appointment books. Whether we head for the hill country or await a visitor, together we wait upon one another. Together we rejoice, celebrate, and hope

After three months, which was just about the time for Elizabeth to give birth, Mary went home. No longer with anxiety and haste: instead I picture a slow, meditative walk out of the hills and back down to the valley. There has been time for her to think through the angelic encounter that would change her life, like a pond that is gradually clearing after a rainstorm. I like to think that her anxieties were lessening, her worries disappearing, with new confidence and hope as clarity is restored. She has been received with love. She has been heard.

Chapter 9

His First Walk

An angel of the Lord appeared to Joseph in a dream and said, "Get up, take the child and his mother, and flee to Egypt, and remain there until I tell you; for Herod is about to search for the child, to destroy him." Then Joseph got up, took the child and his mother by night, and went to Egypt, and remained there until the death of Herod. (Matthew 2:13–15)

Joseph, the practical patron saint of those who work with their hands, from artisans to plumbers, would seem an unlikely dreamer. Daily he crafted the tangible and measurable into the furniture of ordinary life. His eyes had to be keen and his hands strong and steady. His craft demanded that he be bold and cautious at the same time— my woodworking friends tell me that their maxim is "Measure twice and cut once." Under those hands wood became tables and benches, yokes for oxen, and carts for donkeys. I hope that he never had to construct a cross. Probably this would not have required the skill of a master carpenter because anyone could nail two pieces of wood of the right size together, and there was no reason why a suitable cross could not be used over and over. The condemned man would not be needing it again.

Joseph, the generous man who broke the rules of his society by saving Mary from disgrace, is a vital part of the story. As he fled Bethlehem from Herod, he took the infant Jesus on his first walk.

Over the centuries artists have depicted him as old, even a bit doddery. Perhaps a widower, which would have conveniently explained away Jesus' brothers and sisters, gallantly rescuing a young woman in distress and possible danger. It must have been difficult for the church to see Joseph as young or even youngish, virile, and marriageable. In the past few years, however, I have begun to see new depictions of Joseph, not by recognized artists of past centuries nor in museums, but tucked into odd corners of women's religious houses, in which he is tenderly watching the baby while Mary gets a bit of sleep or listening affectionately to a little boy of four or five standing at his side. Joseph, very human and very much a loving father.

But for most of us, the old image is indelibly fixed: he's a kindly septuagenarian. As a practical dreamer Joseph is vital to the story, but definitely second string, usually relegated to the background with the focus centered on Mary and her winsome baby. In our own time he is venerated as the patron of real estate sales: just bury a plastic image of Joseph upside down in your lawn, and your house will sell. Yet like his namesake in the Book of Genesis, this practical man, a worker with his hands, is still a dreamer.

And he clearly trusts his dreams. When he learned—How did he know? Did he just guess? Did Mary confide in him?—that Mary was inexplicably pregnant, he wished to spare her shame and disgrace. Matthew tells us he "planned to dismiss her quietly. But the angel of the LORD appeared to him in a dream and said, 'Joseph, son of David, do not be afraid to take Mary as your wife, for the child conceived in her is from the Holy Spirit'" (Matthew 1:20). I might have been tempted to dismiss the dream, especially since it called for radical action on my part, or at least to argue with the divine messenger, but Joseph recognized the voice of authority and followed instructions.

You know what happens: the baby is born in a stable in Bethlehem with benevolent animals standing by. The skies open to the singing of angels and the message of peace on earth. The shepherds pay homage. A few days later the mysterious astrologers from the east arrive in Bethlehem after trekking across the desert following a star. With their coming this is no longer the story of a humble little family far from home. This is no ordinary baby, but a threat to the established order. The holy story has become political and dangerous as Herod, collaborator with the Roman occupation, fears a rival. So Joseph dreams his second dream: "Herod is out to kill you. Pack up, take the baby and his mother, and get going. Head for Egypt. And stay there until I tell you that the coast is clear!"

My own heart would sink at such a message. What if God's voice came to me in a dream and said, "Gather up what you can carry in your two hands—at least you don't have a squirmy baby to lug—and get out of D.C. Head for Guadalajara! I know that it's a long way and there are a couple of deserts and a few mountains to get through, and you don't speak the language, but this is where you're going. A plane is out of the question, and of course there are no buses, so you'll have to walk. Be careful, though, the government is out to get you!"

I would be baffled by such a dream and tempted to ignore it. Or maybe to seek out a trusted friend or a psychotherapist for a second opinion. Joseph knew better: he had trusted the same imperious voice that came to him in the night nine months ago.

Not only is this a walk commanded in a dream; it is also another departure by night. Even though the departure of the Israelites from Egypt, centuries earlier, was hasty, there was plenty of time to prepare. Moses had been negotiating with Pharaoh for weeks, and even at the last minute there was time for the ritual meal, the prescribed disposal of leftovers, and the ominous but comforting blood markings framing the soon-to-be abandoned doors. The flight of this family from Bethlehem is different: "Run for your life!"

Why Egypt? Why didn't the angel just tell Joseph to go back to where they came from, lie low for a while, and blend into the crowd? Because, Matthew tells us, the goal of the journey was not only to evade Herod but also to fulfill a prophecy: "Out of Egypt I have called my son." He is closing the loop, as it were, connecting two prophecies that identify Jesus as the Messiah. He is the child born to Mary in Bethlehem, and he is the exile who must return from Egypt to Judea: "But you, O Bethlehem of Ephrathah, who are none of the little clans of Judah, from you shall come forth for me one who is to rule in Israel, whose origin is from old, from ancient days" (Micah 5:2). Matthew doesn't tell us whether Joseph had time to reflect on these Old Testament prophecies, but I'm willing to bet that he recognized mortal danger and acted quickly. Maybe he was still pondering the amazing appearance of the magi, and maybe he was wondering what to do with their lavish gifts. Frankincense and myrrh were laden with royal and priestly symbolism; he could think about that later. Mary might have known the healing power of myrrh: if you could afford it, it was a soothing a household remedy for cuts and abrasions.

The long journey into an unknown land was no doubt a practical one: to get out of reach of Herod, to go as far as possible from danger. Yet there is irony in the fact that Egypt was the goal of the journey. As the site of the Israelites' slavery; it is an alien place of uncleanness far, far from home. This is a flight to safety, but at the same time it is yet another embracing of exile.

I have to wonder: did our gospel writer know anything about traveling with babies, babies who would eventually turn in to toddlers if you stayed on the road long enough? Decades ago I packed up and flew to Buenos Aires with a recalcitrant four-year-old and a fairly amiable infant. I wasn't fleeing Herod but simply being a good wife supporting her husband's career. In no way was my departure a flight from danger, but I recall it as a hastily prepared journey into the unknown. We had been on standby for quite a while: the trip had been on, then off, then on again. When the word from on high came, we had to move quickly.

As I moved through strange airports, I asked myself if I would ever walk again in an alien place without holding tight to a small hand while I juggled a wiggly baby on my hip. What would it be like when I got there? Would I find a pediatrician? Would the milk be safe to drink? What about diapers? How on earth did you keep them clean? Would I have a washing machine? Were there strange diseases to creep up on me unawares? My concerns were small; the thought of menace from an angry king never occurred to me. I was just a housewife, and my children were quite ordinary.

To say nothing of the language barrier. Joseph and Mary presumably spoke Aramaic. What on earth did people speak in Egypt? Sign language will get you only so far, but there are times when some subtlety is necessary. The locals can be impatient and dismissive; when they are patient you feel like an awkward child again, finding her way without nuance in a complicated world. I learned this the hard way when necessity compelled me to order groceries by phone in my feeble Spanish. A street with murderous traffic lay between me and the little corner store. It would be hard enough to cross by myself, but carrying the baby and dragging the four-year-old along was impossible. Surprisingly, in my first phone conversation with the friendly grocer, we did well on the basics: bread, apples, milk. But I needed light bulbs. In my halting Spanish I described what I needed: "*Una cosa que hace luz in el cielo*—a thing that makes light in the ceiling." The patient grocer replied, "*Ah, senora, una bomba!*" It was a time of political unrest in the country; (Would the exiled dictator return, or was a new breed of terrorism lurking?) so I protested vigorously, "No bombas! No bombas!" It turned out that he was right all along, the harmless bombas arrived, and there was light in the kitchen. Along with a new word, I had learned a lesson in humility and helplessness, the isolation of being a stranger in a strange land with only a halting command of the language, dependent on the good will and native courtesy of the locals.

But compared to Mary and Joseph carrying their newborn through miles and miles of alien country, I had it easy. What did they manage to bring with them? The gifts of the magi would have enabled them to buy almost anything in the markets, but had there been time? And would it have been prudent to load themselves down with pots and pans and maybe some new carpenter's tools for Joseph? Where did they sleep? Were the strangers they met along the road friendly and patient with them like my grocer? Or were they dismissed harshly: "Why don't you go back where you came from? At least learn to speak the language ! You ought to know that Jews aren't welcome here." Perhaps now and then some Egyptian grandmother couldn't resist: "What a cute baby! What's his name?"

And what did Mary and Joseph talk about? They might have taken turns reassuring themselves, telling and retelling the story: "Yes, that's really what happened!" Or they might have bolstered each other up: "Let me carry the baby for a while. Surely we'll be there before too long. Aren't we lucky that we got away?" And just like the rest of us, they got fed up and grumpy.

One of my favorite pictures in the National Gallery is "Rest on the Flight into Egypt" by Gerard David. It's a lovely scene: a delicate, blonde Mary, beautifully dressed, sits beneath a tree with a serene infant on her knee. She is holding a bunch of grapes before him; his little hand reaches out to pluck one. Joseph is in the background, knocking nuts from a tree. A sturdy donkey is tethered nearby. It looks more like a family outing in the Flemish countryside than a flight through the desert, tipped off by an angel.

I'm pretty sure that it wasn't like that. I hope that they had that donkey; but, if they couldn't even get a room in the inn in Bethlehem, how could they expect to get relatively easy transport out of the country? So I picture them walking. For how long? If the trip lasted long enough, the infant Jesus could have turned into a toddler on the way. Did that slow them down or speed things up? In the way of children, he might have surpassed his parents and picked up some of the basics of the local dialect, which could have been helpful.

But aside from the near miracle of saving her child, that very special child if Gabriel were to be believed, there could have been a cloud over her joy. Matthew doesn't tell us whether Mary and Joseph knew what happened after their hasty departure from Bethlehem: "When Herod saw that he had been tricked by the wise men, he sent and killed all the children in and around Bethlehem who were two years old or under, according to the time that he had learned from the wise men" (Matthew 2:16). What mother could rejoice in the safety of her own child if she knew that his birth had caused the slaughter of countless other children We slide so quickly over December 28, which commemorates these first unwitting Christian martyrs. It's easier to close our eyes and continue to bask in the warm glow of Christmas. But I suspect that Mary knew the story and never forgot it. Did she tell it to her son—too terrible for a bedtime story, but nevertheless part of his own story? Or did she just tuck it away with all the other bits and pieces that she pondered in her heart?

This story ends with another dream and another walk. When Herod dies, the angelic messenger turns up yet again: "It's time to go back home. Start walking. Judea's not a good idea right now, so it's probably safer in Nazareth. No need to carry the boy, He can out-walk both of you by now." And so Jesus resumed his first walk.

So far as I know, God has never given me marching orders in a dream. Maybe I haven't paid attention—not deliberately, of course, but his voice has not been loud enough to wake me up. With age, for better or worse, one sleeps more lightly. There might still be time. Will I snap to attention and put on my shoes? Or will I roll over and feign sleep? After all, Egypt is a long way off, and I have no desire to be a refugee. Besides, I'm not important enough to get Herod's attention.

Chapter 10

A Day Trip
with Consequences

Six days later, Jesus took with him Peter and James and his brother John and led them up a high mountain, by themselves. And he was transfigured before them, and his face shone like the sun, and his clothes became dazzling white. Suddenly there appeared to them Moses and Elijah, talking with him. Then Peter said to Jesus, "Lord, it is good for us to be here; if you wish, I will make three dwellings here, one for you, one for Moses, and one for Elijah." While he was still speaking, suddenly a bright cloud overshadowed them, and from the cloud a voice said, "This is my Son, the Beloved; with him I am well pleased; listen to him!" When the disciples heard this, they fell to the ground and were overcome by fear. But Jesus came and touched them, saying, "Get up and do not be afraid." And when they looked up, they saw no one except Jesus himself alone.
(Matthew 17: 1–8)

Although I have loved walking all my life, I am assuredly not a mountain climber. After all, I am a child of the relatively flat midwest, and gently undulating hills were all we had where I grew up. On visits home nowadays I join forces and walk with my brother, where we join other aging folk to circumnavigate the local mall. It's warm in winter, cool in summer, with little ramps so that those who can't manage steps can move easily down a few feet to a new level. Twice around equals a mile; and three times around is an athletic feat. It is well lit night and day, all obstacles cleared away, goals clearly defined. End up where you intended to go, preferably back where you started. So I am genetically and no doubt temperamentally inclined to avoid steep ascents and precipitous declines; an uneventful walk to Whole Foods or to Joe the dry cleaner, an aimless stroll round the neighborhood, or a trip to the library suits me just fine.

But then I recall this significant story of a walk with Jesus that was so crucial to his ministry and destiny that it was told not once but three times by Matthew, Mark, and Luke, a walk "up a high mountain, by themselves." Jesus was always walking, and he may not have been into casual strolls. He had no office or office hours, so the roads around Palestine were where he worked—encountering, teaching, talking, healing, and no doubt sharing fruitful silence. Even those final days of walking with his friends, headed ultimately toward Jerusalem, can seem unplanned, casual, almost leisurely.

When most of us travel, we want everything carefully mapped out: plane reservations, neatly printed schedules with arrival and departure times, no layovers or detours, knowing exactly who will pick us up at the baggage carousel. I had some hours of panic a few weeks ago, when I feared that I would be stuck in an Alabama airport overnight. Now, when I reflect on my bad mood, I realize that Jesus would maybe have used the wasted time to heal one or two, perhaps outrage the local clergy, and tell a few stories. The gospel writers, especially Luke, make it sound as if he was in no hurry, teaching, enjoying unplanned stops, and making a detour to heal a sick child. He even upsets the religious authorities by strolling through a grain field on the Sabbath and casually picking handfuls for lunch. When we read the gospels, we are fellow travelers with him, invited to come along on the next walk. So when I read, "Six days later, Jesus took with him Peter and James and John, and led them up a high mountain apart, by themselves," I recognize the promise of adventure and come along, at least in my imagination.

I had read this story many times, repeatedly asking myself, "Why these three disciples? Why not the whole bunch, on a kind of business retreat or offsite meeting?" Finally it dawned on me that impulsive, imperfect Peter, James who never gets much to say, and his brother John the beloved, were also chosen to walk with Jesus to Gethsemane on that final night before his arrest. That is why they were singled out for this walk up into the heights.

Was it a command, an invitation, or a little of both? And what about those disciples who were left behind? Perhaps they welcomed a day off. Jesus, after all, must have set them a high standard, so that a day to loll about without demands could be a welcome change. Maybe they slept late or raided an apple orchard, or bathed themselves and their clothes in a nearby stream. Or perhaps they were bored, at loose ends, relying on Jesus to set the agenda for the day. The ones left behind in the valley might have grumbled, "Why them and not me? Peter drops the ball more than the rest of us, so why does he always get chosen? And what's so special about James and John? I thought we were a team, one for all and all for one."

Tradition sets the scene on Mount Tabor, but my inner picture of this walk sets the scene in Jenkins Hollow on a hot August day. Midsummer is not an ideal time to hike up through the abandoned orchard, then weave my way through the wild rose brambles and the tangled honeysuckle to the top of Sam's Ridge. Poison ivy is flourishing, and there are plenty of bugs, those little ones that head straight for your eyes. Merciless burning sun, relieved by the occasional cloudburst or drenching thunderstorm.

No plastic bottles of water, no wholesome trail mix, no hats to avoid the sun, and sandals rather than sturdy boots for these disciples. Footgear is important here. You never know what you might step on—a snake almost invisible in the thick vegetation, a sharp rock, or, from back when my neighbor ran cows on the mountainside, a steaming reminder of their presence. Even on Mount Tabor it was probably a good idea to be well shod and to watch where you put your feet.

Did Peter, James, and John walk walked silently up the mountain, or did they gossip, tell jokes, quiz Jesus about this break in daily routine? Did they have time to take in their surroundings, look back down their path, and admire the view before they were overcome by the brilliant light transforming their friend and teacher? Was the air thin on the mountain, making them light-headed?

When I let myself enter this story, I am reminded of myself at age fifteen spending an interminable week at a church camp, situated by a stagnant lake with not even a modest hill in sight. It was a miserable experience: my piety just didn't measure up to that of my fellow campers. Every evening we would gather and, one by one, were required to recount "the mountain top experience" of the day. One earnest boy declared every evening that he had decided "to give his life to Christ." I was impressed but not surprised: he didn't seem to have much fun the rest of the time, so this may have been his next best choice. I never had the courage to ask him to elaborate, but I was pretty sure that giving my life to Christ wasn't for me—why would Jesus want or need me? After Bobby Joe or Roy or Tommy opened the discussion, assorted girls described their Missouri equivalents of mystical experience, which sounded better than anything I could come up with. Nothing mystical happened to me: I was only aware of the lack of privacy, the fleas hopping around the rough wood of our cabins, imprisonment in an alien place where I didn't speak the language.

I had nothing to say and was too honest to fake it: Jesus clearly hadn't invited me on a walk to a pathetic hillock during the afternoon "free time." He hadn't even shown up to suggest giving the leaders the slip and taking a low-key ramble together down the road. But except for the social discomfort of having nothing holy to add to the evening conversation, I was frankly relieved and hoped that he would ignore me for the rest of the week. As I look back, I wonder: perhaps I couldn't believe that he would invite me to come along with the select inner circle. Perhaps I suspected—and he knew—that I wasn't up to the climb. It was much safer to stay by the mosquito-infested lake. Life in the valley was challenging enough. If a transcendent light had come to blind me and fling me to the ground, I would probably have mistaken it for sunstroke.

But now, after plodding along over decades on short walks round the block, on level sidewalks in familiar neighborhoods, on fairly well-marked roads, I want to go along on the big adventure. Like Peter and his friends I yearn to be overcome by the overwhelming vision of pure light. I am afraid that, also like Peter, I would want somehow to capture the experience with a tasteful brass plaque or unfocused little picture on the cell phone. Like a good tourist or a pilgrim to a holy site, I might want to bring back something. Ashtrays and mugs are easy to pack, don't take up much room, and seem to last forever.

What happened to Jesus' friends when they reached the mountaintop is almost beyond imagination. The Jesus they thought they knew is transformed, transfigured, a blinding vision. Moses and Elijah, representing and embodying the law and the prophets, appear out of nowhere and start a conversation with Jesus. What were they talking about? We don't have a clue, but neither do the disciples. They are overshadowed by a cloud, and then a voice comes from the cloud: "This is my Son, the Beloved; with him I am well pleased; listen to him!" Peter, James, and John weren't around for Jesus' baptism, or they would have heard the same words, but with an added command: "Listen to him!" Implied, of course, is a deeper message: "Pay attention! This is no ordinary walk in the sunshine. If he is transfigured, then you are transformed. You won't be the same again."

I know enough about mountaintops now to yearn for another chance. Command or invitation, the message is hard to ignore. I'll pull on my hiking boots any time I hear the invitation: "Margaret, we're taking the day off. Let's check out the mountain!" But I also know something else: you can't stay there, not even for a night under the stars, because there is a sequel to the walk that is easy to overlook. In my experience, climbing up to Sam's Ridge in midsummer is much easier than walking or sliding down. If I get a little breathless on the steep walk up, tired of the mosquitoes and the entangling honeysuckle, wishing for some sunscreen and a sturdy walking stick, the walk back to the hollow is harder still. Descending the mountain can be even more challenging than the upward climb.

I wonder if Peter, James, and John were silent on the way down, walking behind or ahead of Jesus, or if they chatted and even told jokes to clear the air. I wonder if the impact of this day had hit them yet: if they had never experienced the mountain, the return to the frustrations of ordinary life might be a terrible disappointment. It may have been like those times when my children were young and demanding. Returning home, and not even from a mountaintop day with Jesus but a few hours at the movies, I found them like baby birds, squawking, with beaks wide open, waiting to be fed. The disciples returned to the first-century equivalent of this demanding scenario: a small boy with epilepsy whom the other disciples could not heal. The child is convulsed with seizures, in danger of hurting himself, killing himself. His distraught father must stand by helplessly, witnessing yet again the torment of his son. The disciples who had the day off are also standing by ineffectually, whispering among themselves, wondering what Jesus would do.

Jesus drives out the unclean spirit. The boy is spent, exhausted, "like a corpse," but he is healed. The disciples are reunited, and things are back to normal. Or, at least, a semblance of normality, for on the trip back down the mountain Jesus had commanded his three friends, "Don't tell anyone what happened today, at least not until I have died and risen again." So they didn't, but they had to wonder what on earth he had been talking about. How did they live into the experience of that day? Did they feel privileged, or burdened with a mysterious secret, or both?

The ascent can be tiring, even exhausting, but it is a matter of putting one foot in front of the other. The inevitable return has its own challenges: don't stumble or trip, lean on that handy walking stick, and keep your eye on the path. Don't be surprised if chaos awaits you at home and, despite your day on the mountaintop, you are still limited and helpless. Be prepared to live with secrets and commands that you don't understand, to be silent when you want to shout, to be helpless when you feel ready at last for action. Remember that you rarely travel alone and that you always travel with an expert guide, who lets you slip and slide a bit, even watches with amusement when you lose your dignity and sprawl helplessly on the path.

The walk up the mountain is no casual outing, but it's worth the climb. And an invitation from Jesus is hard to resist.

Chapter 11

Tips for Travelers

Then Jesus called the twelve together and gave them power and authority over all demons and to cure diseases, and he sent them out to proclaim the kingdom of God and to heal. He said to them, "Take nothing for your journey, no staff, nor bag, nor bread, nor money—not even an extra tunic. Whatever house you enter, stay there, and leave from there. Wherever they do not welcome you, as you are leaving that town shake the dust off your feet as a testimony against them." They departed and went through the villages, bringing the good news and curing diseases everywhere. (Luke 9:1–6)

As one who travels a great deal and who stubbornly insists on carrying her own luggage, I am an expert packer. A suit of some sort in a neutral but uninteresting color like black, brown, or navy, preferably a knit. Yes, knits tend to get baggy with age, but they never wrinkle no matter how long how they have been stuffed in a suitcase. A few turtlenecks of various colors to brighten up the baggy suit, a bathrobe that scrunches into nothing when packed, assorted basic toiletries depending on the length of the trip, a tiny alarm clock, a flashlight—retreat houses and conference centers turn into obstacle courses at night—a good whodunit, and I am ready to go. Sometimes I bring along the laptop computer, ostensibly to do a little work during the flight or while the retreatants are pondering my words or taking a nap, but really to slip in a Netflix disc and enjoy a movie after hours when the Great Silence sets in. And of course my cell phone, although I usually end up in places where the reception is terrible, or where there are signs all over forbidding their use. But I take it along just to prove to myself that I am a thoroughly modern traveler, even if I can never remember my own number.

And when I arrive at my destination, my greeter almost always exclaims: "Is that *all* you have?" I smile modestly and enlarge my reputation as one of Jesus' humble foot soldiers. Surely Jesus would have approved of my packing skills, while the twelve would probably have shot me nasty looks for making them look bad. Some travelers are notorious for dragging all sorts of extra stuff, just in case they need it on the way, but Jesus would have been able to send me off without my own special pillow or a hair dryer or an ample supply of bottled water. He might even have persuaded me to let go of the laptop and confiscated my paperback whodunit.

The disciples were about to be sent out with a pretty heavy assignment: to cast out demons, to cure diseases, to heal, and to proclaim the kingdom of God. I'll be the first to admit that on my travels, even though in a modest way I presume to do the work of God, I have it easier—conducting a weekend retreat for hospitable seekers, offering a workshop or preaching at a friendly, presumably demon-free, parish. And I can be assured that I will not go hungry. Instead, just to be polite, I'll break all the rules of my fairly ascetic regular diet and feast on lasagna and high-calorie desserts. After all, Jesus told the disciples to eat whatever is set before you. It would be rude to refuse second helpings or protest that a well-ripened Brie to top off the meal would play havoc with my triglycerides.

Then Jesus goes on to set standards for their luggage: "Take nothing for your journey, no staff, no bag, nor bread, nor money—not even an extra tunic." There go my extra turtlenecks to say nothing of my lightweight bathrobe. I would be inclined to argue or perhaps sneak some extras into my shoulder bag. After all, women always need a purse of handbag or tote bag of some sort. As hewers of wood and drawers of water, it is our role in life always to be lugging something somewhere. So maybe I would get away with tucking in some trail mix, a telescopic umbrella, a credit card, and a twenty dollar bill. I might not declare the credit card, just sneak it past Jesus' scrutiny. Maybe I would even argue that it would be more efficient to bring my laptop and cell phone.. On a mission like this, regular reports of progress (or lack of it) could be useful for future strategic planning.

Of course the disciples were literally walking—no donkey cart on which to load their luggage, no porters to follow behind them while they stepped lightly along, not even the well-designed back packs featured in my L.L. Bean catalog. These were poor people who didn't own much of anything in the first place. Maybe they even chuckled a little when Jesus set forth his standards—"Why is he bothering to tell us this? It's a no-brainer!"

It would be easy to read Jesus' instructions about traveling light as a condemnation of materialism, about our tendency to weight ourselves down so that we can scarcely move. He would be right at home with the current rigid standards for air travel. It seems like only yesterday when travelers would trundle up to the ticket window and blithely check suitcases the size of small refrigerators. As I sit surrounded by all my now fairly shabby treasures, it's comforting to realize that this could equally well have been an issue two thousand years ago in an impoverished corner of the world. Even the disciples had their nets. And they were able to walk away. They were able to trust this charismatic teacher, somehow to walk down the road with him with no idea where they were going.

Jesus saw clearly that the twelve could be dragged down on their walk if they were lugging a lot of stuff. They could forget what they were supposed to be doing if they kept checking on their impedimenta or worrying if their money were running out or wondering if they hadn't left their favorite staff behind when they stopped to rest under that big tree a few miles back. And of course they could even be dragging along intangible baggage, musing and muttering to themselves, "What's left of me? Who on earth am I now, if I can't claim to be a fisherman or even a tax collector any more? I've thrown aside family responsibilities, in fact all my responsibilities, just to go on this walk. If this is what traveling unencumbered means, I'm not sure that I like it!"

But Jesus is demanding more than just freedom from stuff, both tangible and intangible. He's demanding complete trust in himself. No crossed fingers behind your back, no little escape clauses in fine print at the bottom of the contract, no time of grace to think it over before you commit yourself, no negotiations. Let it all go and start walking. Total trust is what it's about. And what may be even harder to accept, total dependence on him.

Just as I can read this story as a lesson of guidance for the frugal packer, it's quite easy to take Jesus' commands literally. Not that this is a bad idea. In our society of abundance, it is easy to accumulate all sorts of things, then come to regard them as true necessities even though we don't know where we picked them up or why we hang on to them. When I lived in New York, one of my great teachers was Pauline, the affluent bag lady. I came to know her well as she frequented the Tuesday Senior Citizens Lunch at the parish where I served. She had a quite pleasant apartment in a safe building, she had traveled the world, she was well educated, but somehow in her old age she had turned into a bag lady.

When she wasn't at the church for lunch, she wandered the streets of Yorkville gathering up junk, like used Styrofoam cups, old newspapers, grocery ads, and menus from Chinese restaurants. When she was about to be evicted as a fire hazard, a friend and I cleaned her apartment, a labyrinth of junk. Pauline understood what we were doing, but she stood by and wept as we—or so it seemed to her— destroyed her security, indeed, her very identity. When we finished, after two days of hard and dirty work, she had a pleasant home. After we removed several cubic feet of detritus, she could even use the bath tub again.

Pauline continues to haunt me, decades later, because she numbers among my most memorable teachers, even if neither of us realized it at the time. I can still see her as a pitiable old woman, eccentric, no doubt mentally ill with a compulsion to hoard. But I realize now that she was compelled to surround herself with all that junk and turn her home into a fortress because she was frightened of a world she no longer knew and because she trusted no one, not even herself. Her towers of tattered coupons and Dunkin' Donuts cups assured her safety in a dangerous and unreliable world. Trust in God was for her at best a piece of sentimental jargon.

Beyond luggage limits, Jesus has a few more rules for the road. He tells his followers, "Don't greet people along the way" (Luke 10:4), and this one baffles me. It just doesn't seem friendly; indeed it's asking for trouble. Commentators on this passage suggest that stopping to chat would cause delay, but this seems a feeble excuse. Jesus wants to be sure that his friends know that they are on a mission, not a casual hike, but a friendly "Hello" now and then wouldn't have taken any time. I would have trouble not stopping to chat a bit, maybe to check the route or admire a child, maybe to ask how far to the next village, maybe just to exchange a few words with a friendly farmer. But this walk is a single-minded, purposeful march. Look forward. Keep walking. Don't let yourself get distracted.

And don't stay where you're not wanted. Jesus tells his friends, "By all means, accept and enjoy hospitality along the road, but if you are not welcomed, go into its streets and say, 'We don't even want the dust of your town sticking to our feet! Don't you know that the kingdom of God has come and you can't even see it?" That's strong language, but why would these hikers want to hang around where they weren't wanted anyway? Fatigue? Worn out and needing a place to stop for the night? Disillusionment, because walking with Jesus had turned out to be such hard and unrewarding work? Perhaps curiosity: "Why aren't we welcome here? After all, even if we look shabby, we're following God's chosen one. Jesus talks about fields ripe for the harvest, and this place looks overripe. Let's hang around and see what happens." But Jesus says, don't stay where you're not wanted. This could be a useful eleventh commandment! But maybe we ordinary folk should leave off the curse that follows: "I tell you, it shall be more tolerable on that day in Sodom than for this town—or household or committee or club or church." So let's leave that judgment to Jesus and just depart quietly.

Along the way an anonymous "someone" by the roadside called out, "I will follow you wherever you go" (Luke 9:57–62). Jesus the realist pointed out that it would not be an easy trip— no motels, no B & Bs, not even a roof over your head. We don't know whether the eager would-be disciple came along anyway. Probably not. I'm ashamed to admit it, but I might have had second thoughts at this point. Long ago on my solitary wanderings in Europe, I traveled happily without reservations; I would simply get off the train in some interesting small town and look for a cheap hotel—no central heating, a primitive bathroom down the hall with a surcharge if you actually took a bath, and a Spartan room with a lumpy mattress that made a monastic cell look luxurious. Now my standards have changed. In even the most austere retreat center I expect a single room with bath and air-conditioning in the summer heat. Even when I try to frame my requests tactfully, even modestly, I can almost see Jesus' amused look. After all, he warned a potential follower who promised to follow him *anywhere*, "Foxes have holes, and birds of the air have nests; but the Son of Man has nowhere to lay his head." I have a long way to go before I measure up. I simply don't want to sleep in holes with the foxes even though it may come to that.

In her heyday I had an ongoing argument with Mother Teresa. She never knew it, so it probably did no harm. I envied her for her single-mindedness, indeed for her recklessness. When she heard the call, she simplified her wardrobe (which no doubt was already pretty austere), signed on with no reservations, and hit the road. Maybe she had reservations, but she no doubt chopped them down like noxious weeds whenever they dared show so much as a tiny sprout. How could she live in the gutters of Calcutta with one sari and a bucket? How could she spend her days with the sick and filthy, with no expectation of reward? I could be that holy too, I kept telling myself, if I didn't have a husband and children and a job and a house and commitment to my parish and on and on. If I didn't like a hot shower every day and clean clothes and good food— not gourmet, of course, just fairly nutritious and unlikely to make me sick. And a clean bed and more books than I could ever read and a certain modest status in the community. And, of course, a lot of friends who didn't think I was crazy.

One of the advantages of age, at least as I am experiencing it, is that stuff doesn't matter nearly so much as I once thought, indeed, as I was reared to value it. Perhaps the great sin of relative affluence is the urge to hoard, to hold on tight if not to acquire more, telling ourselves that prudence like ours could never be greed.

I haven't achieved Jesus' standard of material austerity yet, but I'm working on it. A few years ago it was a real pleasure to dump my grandmother's twelve-place setting of elegant china on my elder daughter. She got more than she bargained for, but she hasn't realized it yet. I'd dragged it around for fifty years without realizing what a burden it was. It couldn't go in the dishwasher, and when would I ever have twelve people trying to sit down at a table, which comfortably seats four? To be sure, I still hang on to my staff and an extra tunic. It seems foolhardy to let them go and who knows when they might come in handy?

Harder still is letting go of the invisible, intangible impedimenta like envy, arrogance, neediness, and fear. Some of them are troubling, some of them feed my ego, some are there just because that's where they have always been. If you drag them with you long enough, you forget how heavy they are. You forget how to run, how to skip, even to walk briskly. You drag them along like Brecht's Mother Courage with her cart and eventually you even forget what it might be like to walk unimpeded.

I comfort myself with the imperfection of the twelve. Like the rest of us, they too remained works in progress to the very end. Maybe I have just one more walk. Everything has been practice up to now.

Chapter 12

A Walk Interrupted

"A man was going down from Jerusalem to Jericho, and fell into the hands of robbers, who stripped him, beat him, and went away, leaving him half dead. Now by chance a priest was going down that road; and when he saw him, he passed by on the other side. So likewise a Levite, when he came to the place and saw him, passed by on the other side. But a Samaritan while traveling came near him; and when he saw him, he was moved with pity. He went to him and bandaged his wounds, having poured oil and wine on them. Then he put him on his own animal, brought him to an inn, and took care of him. The next day he took out two denarii, gave them to the innkeeper, and said, 'Take care of him; and when I come back, I will repay you whatever more you spend.' Which of these three, do you think, was a neighbor to the man who fell into the hands of the robbers?" (Luke 10:30–36)

I very much dislike my walks to be interrupted. Even if it is a walk with no fixed destination, just a stroll or a hike around the neighborhood to stretch my legs and clear the cobwebs from my head, I have a purpose and dislike being distracted. But even more annoying is an interruption when I am in a hurry, when I am making a quick run to the grocery store or hurrying to keep an appointment. I have organized my day down to the last minute, and there is no place for casual detours or for a dead stop. Once the walk begins, I want to finish it.

What about the walkers Luke tells us about in the familiar story of the Good Samaritan? We could just as easily call it the story of the hapless victim or the preoccupied priest and Levite. We don't know what kind of business has taken them from Jerusalem to Jericho, but it had to be something important. After all, these two are important people, pillars of society. The Levite, a lay associate of the priest, was the designated expert in the minutia of worship and, like the priests, dedicated to God's service. Like the priests, his role was also hereditary— you didn't just decide to grow up and be a priest or a Levite as you might choose to be a lawyer or a broker. But the story isn't named for them; they just pass by, absorbed in their own affairs. Instead it bears the name of the outcast, the despised, the Samaritan. In our own time, we would have to call it the story of the "good terrorist" or the "good illegal" in order to get the full impact, because it is important to remember that the Samaritan didn't fit, didn't belong on the scene. He was the despised and discounted other.

And it is also a story about three journeys down what seems to be a questionable route. I've never walked that road, but I know it would have been downhill from Jerusalem to the valley of the Jordan. It was a notoriously dangerous road, with deserted stretches when a solitary traveler was extremely vulnerable; a robber could make quick work of his victim and then withdraw to wait for another. We don't know why the nameless traveler was robbed, beaten, and left to die beside the road. He might have been wealthy, or at least well-off, hence worth robbing. He was simply in the wrong place at the wrong time. It was not enough to grab his money and whatever else he might have been carrying. He was beaten savagely and left to die.

His fellow travelers on the road to Jericho are purposeful people of the professional class who know better than to let their journey be interrupted. Maybe they were so engrossed in thinking about their affairs that they simply did not notice the battered man by the roadside. Maybe they decided that he was already dead and thus ritually unclean; that was reason enough to pass by on the other side. Or perhaps they had very tight schedules and couldn't risk being late.

I really don't want to identify with them. Despite their fine credentials the priest and Levite are cold-hearted and self-absorbed, insulated against the hurts of the world. And if they are ignorant of the suffering around them, nearly blocking their path on the way to Jericho, who can blame them for not stopping? They're not bad people, indeed they are no doubt pillars of society. Who can blame them if they have important business to attend to, are pressed for time, simply don't notice the wounded man in their path?

Then comes the Samaritan. He might have been walking, leading his laden donkey, or he might have been riding. Either way, he noticed. Regardless of priorities, he willingly interrupted his journey. Not only is this a story of walks interrupted, it is a poignant story of impromptu roadside hospitality: he dressed the wound of the battered man, hoisted him onto the donkey, found him shelter, and assured himself that he would receive care. Only then did he continue his walk.

Remember that Samaritans and Jews despised one another. Samaritans were considered a distinct ethnic and religious group who lived in Samaria, originally the northern capital of the kingdom of Israel. Huge tensions existed between the two groups, and no ambitious Jewish father would say to his promising child: "Work hard, get good grades, and maybe you can grow up to be a Samaritan." He would be far more likely to say, "Stick to your own kind and make us proud someday."

Our well-planned walks can easily be interrupted, not only by thieves and robbers but by other unexpected assaults on our carefully planned lives. One minute you are walking blithely down the road, not overburdened by useless, heavy luggage but armed with a good credit card or a generously filled wallet. The trip is carefully planned: lunch at noon at a pleasant wayside inn, arrival just in time for dinner at a nice hotel or the home of a friend. These are the most pleasant walks of our lives—no uncertainties, the weather is lovely, and we feel good, full of energy and happy to be on the way. One summer I was on a walk like that, on my way to visit family and then spend a week teaching at a Benedictine monastery in the midwest. It is something that I do every summer; each visit is a kind of double homecoming with my biological and spiritual families. But then I was interrupted, not by robbers but by a freak accident, and fortunately for me, not left to die. I was not cared for by a passing Samaritan, but a state-of-the-art hospital that saved my life.

Grateful as I was for my good care, I couldn't help mourning my interrupted journey. I hadn't arrived where I wanted to be. I had missed the high point of my summer. But I wasn't dead, and I wasn't lying in the road, battered and bruised, waiting for someone, anyone, to interrupt a journey to save my life.

Now as I look back, I am almost grateful for the interruption. The months of recuperation that I perceived as lost had their own special gifts. I was walking too fast! Just as I can admire nature's seemingly insignificant gifts—small moths, odd pebbles, weeds—when I amble down the road in Jenkins Hollow, this forced interruption, followed by a period of moving slowly and tentatively, showed me a whole new world. Not literally: I already knew every square foot of my apartment. But spiritually I explored places that I had never been before.

My story is an extreme example. I'll be happy when it fades from my immediate consciousness and joins all the other old stories rattling around in my brain. But our shortest walks can be interrupted, indeed assaulted, by unexpected catastrophes. The path seems clear, the day is bright, and then we find ourselves lying wounded and abandoned by the roadside. Bereavement, disappointment, betrayal by those whom we trust, the death of relationships—all kinds of losses, tangible or intangible, can leave us bleeding by the wayside. Jesus' message seems to be: "Don't worry if there are detours on your walk. More to the point, don't worry if you take your eyes off the road and notice the suffering around you. And don't worry if you interrupt the walk to take tender care of that bruised, hurting bundle of rags by the roadside. There is plenty of time for your walk; after all, the schedule is pretty loose. You'll get where you're going soon enough."

I can't help wondering. When Jesus tells this story of the Samaritan, is he, well in advance, identifying with the beaten man left to die in the ditch? After all, he was on the road to Jerusalem and he had predicted to his friends that he would be killed there. He probably knew how he would be killed as well—possibly by assassination, but much more likely by execution at the hands of the Roman occupiers. He knew that he would be bruised and battered and hung on a cross, with many onlookers and many more passing by, where no one stopped to help him.

Chapter 13

Turning Around

There was a man who had two sons. The younger of them said to his father, "Father, give me the share of the property that will belong to me." So he divided his property between them. A few days later the younger son gathered all he had and travelled to a distant country, and there he squandered his property in dissolute living. When he had spent everything, a severe famine took place throughout that country, and he began to be in need. So he went and hired himself out to one of the citizens of that country, who sent him to his fields to feed the pigs. He would gladly have filled himself with the pods that the pigs were eating; and no one gave him anything. But when he came to himself he said, "How many of my father's hired hands have bread enough and to spare, but here I am dying of hunger! I will get up and go to my father, and I will say to him, 'Father, I have sinned against heaven and before you; I am no longer worthy to be called your son; treat me like one of your hired hands.'" (Luke 15: 11–19)

Nowhere in Scripture have I found a message that tells us to stay put and all will be well. That mobility, that need to be on the move, that stepping reflex possessed by even the smallest infant, seems to decree: these feet were made for walking, so get going. You may take a wrong turn, but you've got to set out on your own.

In my younger days I must have been an unlovable child because I was harshly judgmental of all delinquents (although unaware of my own sneaky delinquencies) and nowhere was I more certain of the right path than in this story of the prodigal son. When I first heard this story, long ago in Mrs. Kunzman's third-grade Sunday school class, I heartily disapproved of this young man—what had he been thinking of and why did his father give in so easily? Why didn't he say, "Settle down, and try to be more like your brother." Or, "Yes, you're going to inherit quite a fortune some day, but not while I'm still alive, and certainly not until you know how to handle money." Or, for that matter, "Until you learn what a hard day's work is and find a nice girl and settle down, you just stay put!" In my limited and somewhat cowardly view I was sure that if only that headstrong younger son had been more like his responsible big brother and just stayed home, he would have avoided a lot of grief. Which, of course, he would have. But at what cost?

Now I am not so sure. Did the younger son have to leave home? Can there be no joyous homecoming without a departure? He did not flee from slavery, he was not exiled, he was not expelled from paradise, but something impelled him to leave certainty and comfort to walk into the uncertainty, indeed misery, of that distant country. Of course the son wasn't anticipating misery. Maybe he could not even articulate it to himself, let alone to his father, but he was looking forward to a new life of adventure and autonomy. In other words, he was growing up. His father doesn't even seem surprised, although he surely would have preferred that his headstrong child would emulate his steadier older brother.

When I remember myself at twenty-one I can begin to understand this younger son. I had won a modest scholarship to study for a year in Europe, a rare privilege in 1950. I had never been anywhere completely on my own, and I had never been anywhere where exotic languages were the *lingua franca*. And the very idea of crossing the Atlantic on the Queen Elizabeth was mind-boggling. I went with my parents' somewhat reluctant blessing and their promise to supplement the meager stipend as needed. But be sure to write, and don't wander around alone at night in strange cities! I wrote faithfully but also did quite a lot of wandering. In the end I did not end up in rags among the pigs, but I had grown up.

Conforming and conservative child of a conforming and conservative family, I had felt that irresistible urge to step out on my own, to claim my adulthood. Surely this younger son was not expecting misery any more than I did. Perhaps he just wanted to grow up and live his own life.

He was not necessarily seeking the right path, but so far as he was concerned, at this point any path would do so long as it led to somewhere else. I'm quite happy that my own three children lacked his sense of adventure—or his greed and yearning for self-destruction. And for that matter, where was his mother? Maybe if she had been able to put in an admonitory word or two, the story might have been much shorter and less interesting.

Jesus doesn't provide the details of the conversation between father and son when the latter asks for his inheritance. Was the father surprised? Angry? Disappointed, maybe wondering if he had spoiled his younger child, been too indulgent? Could he help comparing his two sons, even if he didn't say so? And I would like to know how the younger son launched this conversation! Boldly or tentatively, expecting to be turned down? I assume that once the prodigal had his money he went off on foot, perhaps a great distance, but that he was well-shod and had a wad of bills safely tucked away somewhere on his person. Cocky and full of energy, he had the world figured out. I suspect that the young adventurer had contempt for his more staid older brother and a patronizing affection for his generous old fogey of a father who had proved to be such a soft touch. Getting hold of his legal inheritance had been surprisingly easy!

So he leaves the home place with a spring in his step, abundant resources, and confident that he already knows how it is all going to turn out.

I don't know how long he lingered in that far country. Probably it was fun at first; he would have been popular, a heavy spender in the first-century equivalent taverns and fashionable watering holes, with girls hovering around him like flies around a honey pot. At some point, however, his good clothes became filthy and shabby, stained with food and wine, and his sandals wore out. He became pitiable and broke. This son had never pictured himself a menial laborer, but a job as a hired hand began to look good. Lacking the experience to do anything else, he looked after a farmer's hogs out in the country, which for Jews were the ultimate unclean animals. God had made this very clear to Moses and all the Israelites. Swine generally get a bad rap in Scripture. I'm rather fond of them as intelligent animals, although I confess that I haven't known any up close and personal for a long time. Years ago my neighbor in Jenkins Hollow kept a friendly pig just across the road from my house. She was a beautiful pedigreed Poland China, so I named her Ludmilla. She would snort at me when I contributed my meager but nutritious garbage to her supper and I would snort back. We were friends of a sort, but we both knew our place in the great order of God's economy. Ludmilla had a certain refinement, even dignity. I suspect that the pigs that the son looked after were less refined than she, and reeked to high heaven. Still, at least he had some shelter; cut off from family and friends, he was at home with them. In a way, they were a kind of surrogate family. He stank, but that no doubt helped him fit in with the herd.

Scripture doesn't tell us how long he sojourned with the hogs. But it was a time of immobility, physical and spiritual. The prodigal was no longer walking anywhere, but mired down in the reeking muck and very alone. Where were those people who had befriended him, admired him, and exploited him when he had arrived in the far country with his pockets full of money? Where were the fellow journeyers in his life?

Twelve Step programs refer to "bottoming-out" as the turning point, when the afflicted one realizes that life has become unbearable and that drastic change is in order for survival. The theological word for this process is "metanoia," meaning repentance, a 180-degree turn in order to redirect one's steps. Jesus put it more simply: the younger son, he tells us, "came to himself." He has become aware. He can look at himself and truly see himself. This had to be an excruciating experience. It was also the first real step on his journey: now, filled with shame but with his vision restored, he can go home. All else has been prologue, stage-setting. What follows is the real walk.

He has taken the wrong path. Now he must redirect his steps and get it right. This appears to be an inevitable part of the human condition, the long walk between life's thresholds. The way ahead had seemed clear, promising freedom and all sorts of good things. The ne'er-do-well younger son must have felt quite free once he cast off the baggage of family life with its obligations, now that he no longer needed the support and love of those who care for him. He could show that elder brother a thing or two while he enjoys that walk away from home without a backward glance.

But then "he came to himself"—another way of saying that his vision was restored. It must have been like waking up and recovering from a terrible hangover. He knew that there was only one way to survive and that was to go home. To reverse the journey, to walk the same road again, this time in shame and uncertainty.

The walk home must have seemed twice as long as it really was. I can picture his feet, cracked and sore, so that each step must have hurt. It was bad enough to be ragged, dirty, and hungry, but his anxiety must have been still worse. Maybe his father wasn't such a soft touch as he remembered. Or might his father have died while he was gone, and his older brother, who lived by the rules and had never yielded to a foolish impulse, been put in charge? Worst of all, as he anticipated his reception, was the flood of shame. Adam and Eve were the first to experience it in Eden when they realized that they were naked. Shame is worse than guilt, and even more devastating. Usually we can do something about guilt—apologize, make amends, accept punishment, or grovel as a last resort. But shame is like a stubborn virus. It takes us over, moves in to stay. We cannot bear even to look at it.

The son knew what he was going to say. Maybe he practiced it over and over, like a mantra, or turned the words into a marching chant: "I have sinned against heaven and before you; I am no longer worthy to be called your son." Left, right, left, right, over and over. Maybe he turned them into a repetitive prayer, like the Jesus Prayer of the eastern Orthodox tradition, and whispered the words over and over until they became part of him.

The end of the walk was homecoming: "But while he was still far off, his father saw him and was filled with compassion; he ran and put his arms around him and kissed him" (v. 20). He clothed his son in new robes, put a ring on his finger and sandals on his feet. He even persuaded the older son to come to the party. For that is what homecoming is—a lavish feast, with everyone clean and elegantly dressed, and with no place for shame.

Chapter 14

No Turning Back

"When the days drew near for him to be taken up, he set his face to go to Jerusalem." (Luke 9:51)

There is a firmness, a finality to this phrase, "setting one's face." Two memories come to me as I let these few words play in my memory. In the first I couldn't have been more than four years old, a conforming little girl who above all else wanted to be good, beyond reproach. I can't remember the incident, but I can still hear my mother's voice as she said to me, "You're as stubborn as a little mule." Obviously I had set my face in the wrong direction and refused to turn back. At this accusation I burst into tears, feeling unjustly maligned. But today I realize that I am indeed stubborn as a now grown up, senior mule. Throughout my life, I have always felt it just a matter of setting my face in a certain direction, even though I don't always get it right.

The second memory goes back not so many decades ago. It was a winter night, and it was time to go to the hospital for the birth of my much-wanted son. But when I arrived, I heard a persistent voice in my head: "I'm not sure I'm up to this. This is not going to be a fun evening. I'm not so sure now that I even need another child! Maybe I can turn around." But of course, I couldn't. There was no turning back. I had set my face, would miss my dinner, and in a few hours greet the newest member of the family, to whom I murmured, "You're the funniest looking kid I ever saw."

And now another memory pops up. Even though I associate it with rather staid parties in the church "social room" of my childhood, I never connected it with Scripture until now. I wonder if little kids still play musical chairs or, as we called it in my childhood, "Going to Jerusalem"? Round and round the line of chairs we went until the pianist suddenly stopped playing and we had to fling ourselves onto a chair. Since we were always one chair short, a brief scuffle ensued before one unfortunate child had to leave the game and slink away in defeat through no fault of her own. Another chair removed, the music starts again, the march resumes, and another loser doesn't make it to Jerusalem. So on and on until there was only one chair—that was Jerusalem. But it still was just a big bare room in the church basement. No prizes at the end. No real challenge. Certainly no danger, and not much of a trip.

Who, I used to wonder, would want to go to Jerusalem anyway? And, as I doggedly played the tedious game, where was the passion, tenacity, downright stubbornness of my young determined self? Winning or losing in this game without a real goal didn't matter. Certainly our marching round and round in a narrowly circumscribed space bore no resemblance to Jesus' lifelong journey or to the tenacity of Jesus, when he finally set his face toward Jerusalem. His was a long hard walk toward a cruel death. Hardly a game, even though he continued to baffle and provoke the religious authorities along the way. Even Herod was nervous. Who was this upstart, this threat to his reign who had come out of nowhere?

Was Jesus' walk chosen? Not chosen? Either way, truly setting one's face requires a decision, a saying "yes" to a journey into the unknown. Or, for Jesus, into the known. At least some of the time we ordinary folk get it wrong and march resolutely in the wrong direction. We may just keep walking, or we may have the good sense to turn around and start over. But for Jesus there was no turning back. To set his face toward Jerusalem was a long walk toward his crucifixion, and he seemed to know how it would end. Judging by my own low standards, he was stubborn, deeply committed to his messianic calling, or just plain foolhardy. Maybe all three. After all, he could have stayed home and been a fine, beloved rabbi. Or a skilled carpenter and a pillar of the community.

This was not his first walk to Jerusalem. As a twelve-year old Jesus had gone with Mary and Joseph on their annual Passover pilgrimage. He must already have accompanied them on previous years, but this time is different because he is growing up. He is no longer a little boy, but on the brink of adolescence, when he eludes Mary and Joseph to stay behind. His anxious parents find him in the temple calmly sitting among the teachers, listening to them and asking them questions. It seems almost like a dress rehearsal for that dramatic, pivotal moment in his ministry, when Jesus resolutely redirects his steps and his life and returns to the holy city.

As a popular teacher and healer, his ministry is well underway before that climactic moment when he set his face toward Jerusalem. Jesus has already managed to outrage the establishment, beginning with a "local boy makes good" return to his home town of Nazareth. When he teaches in the synagogue, the people who had known him all his life are amazed by his wisdom: "Can this be Joseph's boy?" But then he goes too far, Luke tells us, and they try to kill him. Miraculously he escapes and takes to the road. Luke doesn't give us his schedule or itinerary, but it is clear that Jesus has a growing reputation; he is a celebrity, a star with a faithful following. At least part of the attraction must have been his willingness to break the rules and outrage the establishment, including the fact that (like many a celebrity since) he seemed to relish it. So it is no wonder that, before long, the Pharisees take a growing interest in him. This is no gentle Jesus meek and mild, but an attractive, bold, provocative young man. When he heals the paralyzed man, lowered by his friends through the roof, he says, "Your sins are forgiven." The Pharisees are outraged: "Who are you to forgive sins?" Jesus' reply sounds rather offhand, or at least dismissive: "It's all pretty much the same thing as saying 'Get up and walk.'"

Even worse, he is attracted to all the wrong people, enjoying their company and even eating with them. So when he encounters Matthew, a tax collector, he invites him, "Come and follow me." Matthew joins him and hosts a great feast, to which all the other tax collectors are invited. I'm fairly sure that nowadays, professionally at least, tax collectors may not be generally loved, but they are not despised and ostracized. Most of them are reasonably respectable citizens, church members, and pillars of the community. (I speak as one who has a nephew who works for the Internal Revenue Service: he's a decent person with a steady government job, not a crook or an oppressor of the poor.) But in Jesus' day they were despised as dishonest, greedy, collaborators with the hated Roman rulers. Surely no little boy in first-century Palestine announced to his parents, who were hoping to bring up a farmer or a good, honest carpenter, "I want to grow up and be a tax collector!"

Also to the Pharisees' disapproval, Jesus takes a far too casual and practical attitude toward the Sabbath. Out in the country with his disciples, as Luke tells the story, they are hungry and find they haven't any food. So they help themselves to some handfuls of grain from a field and eat. The Pharisees show up and catch them in the act. Jesus and his friends have willfully disregarded the prohibition against working on the Sabbath. His response to their disapproval? "The Son of Man is lord of the Sabbath"—or "So what? We were hungry. Food was here. Why not eat?"

Now the drama moves toward the last act. His journey and his work go on seemingly unchanged, but the focus has narrowed and sharpened. I wonder if the disciples felt the change, if they grasped that everything up to now had been prologue, the easy part. They seem remarkably obtuse much of the time. Jesus knew how the story would end, but did they? Life is easier when we live in denial. Maybe Jesus wasn't really serious about that business of taking up one's cross daily, they said among themselves And why would he insist on marching steadily toward a terrible death?

The walk stops short outside Jerusalem. No more walking now. The small town carpenter reveals himself as a bold, masterful showman. And he knows his scripture too, recalling Zechariah's prophecy of long ago:

⚜

> *Rejoice greatly, O daughter Zion!*
> *Shout aloud, O daughter Jerusalem!*
> *Lo, your king comes to you;*
> *triumphant and victorious is he,*
> *humble and riding on a donkey,*
> *on a colt, the foal of a donkey.* (Zechariah 9:9)

⚜

As a little kid, I wondered why the story couldn't end right here. I can't remember a single Palm Sunday in my childhood when it rained or was even cloudy. Spring had come, and the story was joyful. The sun was shining on the road to Jerusalem, just as it was shining in Kansas City. The crowds lining the road were happy, tossing flowers and leafy branches every which way, throwing their good clothes down in the road for the donkey to walk on. Jesus had won! He set his face toward Jerusalem, and he triumphed. The long walk was over.

My own experiences of "setting my face" are trivial in comparison. For one thing, my goals—even when I think them worthy and carefully thought out—tend to turn into way stations. For example, I will learn to play the piano. Which I did, in a workman-like way, hitting all the right notes but never really producing music. I'll conquer academe and emerge with an impressive degree. Which I did, but now I can't find my elegant diploma. I'll marry and have children. Which I did, but much as I cherish every one of the last fifty-four years, I know that there is much more to life than that. I'll storm the church and become a priest, back when women priests were a rarity. I'll write a book. I'll lose ten pounds. And so on.

Jesus seems to have set his face only once. He knew where he was going and how the story would turn out. He knew that the walk was much more than simply putting one foot in front of the other. But he set his face and did not look back.

So now it's maybe time for me to figure out where I am going. What really matters. Where the real walk is leading. Unlike Jesus, I'm not sure what the end of the road looks like, but I know that it is time to set my face in earnest.

I am still learning a few things about the practicalities— or better, the realities—of the walk. Carefully worked-out schedules aren't to be trusted. An occasional detour is fine. After all, Jesus turned aside to heal a sick child. Now and then it won't hurt to get stuck in an airport overnight; it might be an occasion for adventure or even blessing. Sharing a meal with a few disreputable outcasts can only be enriching. Don't be scared or overly impressed by the occasional nay-sayer; if people disapprove, it must mean that you are doing something right. It is nice to share the walk with friends, but important to remember that we are all just travelers plodding toward our own Jerusalem. I can be pretty sure that when the piano stops, no one is going to yank my chair away.

Chapter 15

Just a Few Steps

They came to Jericho. As he and his disciples and a large crowd were leaving Jericho, Bartimaeus son of Timaeus, a blind beggar, was sitting by the roadside. When he heard that it was Jesus of Nazareth, he began to shout out and say, "Jesus, Son of David, have mercy on me!" Many sternly ordered him to be quiet, but he cried out even more loudly, "Son of David, have mercy on me!" Jesus stood still and said, "Call him here." And they called the blind man, saying to him, "Take heart; get up, he is calling you." So throwing off his cloak, he sprang up and came to Jesus. Then Jesus said to him, "What do you want me to do for you?" The blind man said to him, "My teacher, let me see again." Jesus said to him, "Go; your faith has made you well." Immediately he regained his sight and followed him on the way. (Mark 10:46–52)

S cripture makes it clear that the unlikely or unexpected walk with Jesus cannot be planned far in advance. Indeed, to follow him down the road or up the mountain or into the desert demands the gift of impulsiveness, a certain abandon that does not come easily to the prudent or cautious. After all, we think, we have a lot to lose. What if we get it wrong? As a fairly cautious person, I find it easy to identify with those who yearn to follow Jesus but need to get their affairs in order first, if only to give themselves time to think it over. So I have real sympathy for the unnamed men in Luke's gospel who were ready to follow him anywhere, but needed just a little time to go back and bury a dead father, or say good-bye to the folks at home. By Jesus' standards that simply wasn't good enough and they were left behind. The earliest disciples got it right. When Jesus said, "Follow me," they jumped up, left their nets, didn't go home to tell their wives what they were doing, and simply took off.

"As he and his disciples and a large crowd were leaving Jericho. . . ." How many of these stories of walks with Jesus begin with his coming into a new place or leaving an old one? Some day when I should be doing something else, writing a lecture or doing the laundry, I will sit down and count them. In the meantime I am struck by his always being on the way, being met or being followed, seemingly by chance.

And Scripture hardly ever tells us what the road looks like. It wouldn't do much good to go to Jericho now, as the road is probably a four-lane highway, perhaps with checkpoints or lined with high-rise housing developments. Or running through olive groves.

In my imagination I sometimes place this story on the dirt road that runs past my house in Jenkins Hollow, even though it's much too small to accommodate the crowd described by Mark. Besides, Route 600 doesn't really go anywhere. But it's easy to picture Jesus walking along it on a hot summer day, surrounded by his friends, his fans, the merely curious. At other times I place this story in New York, on Amsterdam Avenue in the west Nineties before it became stylish and dotted with Starbucks. That's the kind of street that attracts crowds, including snappily dressed young professionals, nannies with strollers occupied by the children of the young professionals, homeless people welcoming a diversion on an otherwise ordinary day, Columbia students, tourists. All kinds of voices are in the air—Hispanic dialects, Chinese, the old New York accent still tinged with Yiddish , ordinary Middle American. All talking and yelling at once. Some are not even sure who Jesus is, but they've heard his name and any celebrity is interesting on an otherwise dull day.

At first glance, Mark's story about the blind beggar, who is sitting by the roadside and waiting for Jesus to pass by, seems to have little to do with us. By twenty-first century standards, Bartimaeus is scarcely worth noticing. You get used to seeing him sitting on the sidewalk at his accustomed corner, maybe even exchange a few words as you pass by, maybe drop a few coins or stuff a dollar bill into his hand. Nowadays he's just a blemish on the landscape, pitiful or repellent according to the hardness of your heart, but in his own time he could have been seen as an opportunity for blessing; the laws set forth in Leviticus and Deuteronomy make clear the obligation of the well-off to care for the destitute. So he might have been tolerated, even welcome as a familiar part of the landscape.

But I cannot help moving the story into my own time and place, with their own values and prejudices—a dingy street in a rundown part of New York, an aging suburban strip mall, or perhaps to the busy avenue where I walk every day. As he sits by the road, Bartimaeus is a blemish on the landscape. He does not pull his own weight. He is a parasite, dependent on the casual charity of those citizens who toss him a coin now and then or offer him some leftover food just to keep body and soul together.

I meet Bartimaeus almost every time I walk to Wisconsin Avenue, my nearby shopping street. Sometimes a man, sometimes a woman, Bartimaeus is always living on the edge. I have learned that it is dangerous to stop and talk to him: once you have learned a name, you are compelled to see a person. Depending on your viewpoint, it's downhill or uphill from there. To Edna, who haunts the space in front of Starbucks, I'm "Sweetie." She is bothered on the days when I use my cane— "You don't need that, Sweetie. Just walk!" Tyrone hangs out just across the street near Best Buy and treats me as if I were his favorite grandmother. I've come to expect bear hugs, and I find myself introducing my friends to him, the same way I would want them to know my friends at church. Others along the avenue come and go, but Tyrone and Edna are fixed points in my landscape.

Bartimaeus seems to be a known quantity in the crowd by the roadside waiting for Jesus, tolerated until he begins to make a nuisance of himself. Beggars and other throwaway people should be grateful that they are allowed simply to be. But Bartimaeus has the *chutzpah* to start yelling, "Jesus, Son of David, have mercy on me!" He knows who Jesus is, calls him by his right name. Clearly he is motivated by more than curiosity—he *wants* something. He is probably not sure what he deeply wants, only the hope that restoration of his sight will allow him to see the world for the first time.

His shouting isn't tolerated. He has forgotten his place, and the crowd tries to hush him up. But Jesus hears him. He stops, stands still. This is one of the features of the walk that I overlooked for years, decades. Jesus could just as easily have deputized one of the disciples: "Go back and see what he wants." Or he might even have yelled back to Bartimaeus, "Walk along with me if you can keep up; my schedule is pretty tight today."

Or Jesus might simply have ignored him, just as most of us would be tempted to do. After all, he had to get to where he was going, with all the multitudes to heal or feed or teach. There might have been important people, scribes and Pharisees, waiting for a good debate. Maybe he just couldn't take on one more needy person right now. But even ignoring is hard if the one calling out refuses to give up. I remember myself, a few years ago in Beijing. It was winter, and there were few tourists on the streets. I stood out: a westerner, a woman, alone and old. So I attracted all sorts of folk who wanted "to practice their English" and could walk faster than I, so there was no escape. My last resort was "*Leider spreche ich kein Englisch!*" That worked until I met someone who wanted to practice his German, but I still refused to stop.

But Jesus does. He focuses his complete attention on Bartimaeus. Even if the story ended here, it would provide a good lesson for those of us who see ourselves as his generous, caring followers. There is irony, even humor in the reaction of the crowd when Jesus says, "Call him here." Suddenly they can't do enough to be helpful: "Take heart, get up, he is calling you!" The cynic in me suspects that they are relieved to be getting rid of him—he's Jesus' problem now.

Bartimaeus' walk with Jesus begins here, for this is a story about two walks. Jesus, despite his single-minded command to his followers not to turn aside from their walk ("Salute no one on the road") interrupts his own. And Bartimaeus takes just a few steps on his new path.

He throws off his cloak. This small phrase is easy to miss. The cloak was probably old, frayed, and crusty with dirt and dust., perhaps his only shelter against cold and rain. Here by the roadside, when stumbling to his feet to get to Jesus before he changes his mind, Bartimaeus may have gotten entangled in his cloak. Or maybe he is already looking forward to better days when he will be better dressed. But whether it is a treasure or impediment, he doesn't need it anymore. He has to move quickly to get to Jesus in time. He hasn't heard Jesus' injunction to his followers to let go of everything that weighed them down so that they could travel light, but he knew instinctively that this garment—sheltering or confining, valuable or just rags— was no longer needed. It could slow him down, and he was ready to move.

I suspect that all of us have some equivalent of Bartimaeus' cloak—not a piece of fabric, grand or tattered, but something less tangible that offers shelter, comfort, security, or concealment.

Something like the tattered teddy bear or the frayed old crib sheet that toddlers need to hold onto if the world is to feel safe. Or the magic cloak of invisibility, the stuff of folklore and Harry Potter movies. Dragging any of these around can be more trouble than it's worth. We can get all tangled up and unable to step out boldly. Even when it's time to cast it off, I'm tempted to hold onto a corner, surreptitiously of course, just in case. Bartimaeus has no such inhibitions. He still can't see his path, but he's ready to go.

All along, Bartimaeus has been identified by his blindness and probably defines himself that way. He literally can't see, so no wonder that he also lacks vision in a deeper sense. Yes, Jesus healed broken, impaired, and suffering bodies, but he did not stop there; even those of us with all five senses unimpaired can be blind, deaf, mute, or paralyzed. So, more broadly and deeply, I can read this as a story of spiritual lack of vision, of the inability or unwillingness to see what really matters. I doubt that my very competent ophthalmologist could recognize and diagnose this kind of blindness even though he's very good at upping my prescription and assuring me that I will someday get used to my bifocals.

The walk has begun, but Bartimaeus has to pass one more test: he must say what he truly wants. I would be tempted to look at the ground and stammer, "Sorry to bother you. . . . I know that you are very busy, Jesus, so whatever you think." But to sign on for the walk demands that we say what we need from Jesus: "My teacher, let me see again." Only then can we begin to pull our own weight, work with clarity and confidence, walk with clear vision instead of shuffling along watching our feet.

I never reflect on this story without a bit of surprise at the ending. The walk began with just a few steps—five yards, ten yards, hardly more. But the last two sentences provide the punch line. "Go your way," Jesus says. "Your faith has made you well."

Bartimaeus could have gone back to Jericho, eyes wide open and with a spring in his step. After all, a new day had dawned. He could finally see what his neighbors looked like, be awed by the color of the sky and the fields, been disgusted with the sight of filth and ugliness that up to now he had been spared. He could have gotten some decent clothes, a real job, opened a compassionate, non-profit center to care for the visually impaired. Or he could have hung out at the local watering place, entertaining the whole neighborhood with the story of his own personal miracle. Instead, Mark tells us, "Immediately he regained his sight and followed him on the way."

Bartimaeus took the next steps and never looked back. Maybe we are only free when we see as clearly as he did in that moment. Maybe we fail to notice, even in retrospect, those seemingly insignificant steps that begin the walk.

Chapter 16

Dead Man Walking

Then they led him out to crucify him. They compelled a passer-by, who was coming in from the country, to carry his cross; it was Simon of Cyrene, the father of Alexander and Rufus. Then they brought Jesus to the place called Golgotha (which means the place of a skull). And they offered him wine mixed with myrrh; but he did not take it. And they crucified him, and divided his clothes among them, casting lots to decide what each should take. (Mark 15:20–24)

What is hard for me to remember or accept is that Jesus knew exactly how his life would end. As they moved about the countryside together, teaching and healing, he reminded his disciples twice, "I have to go to Jerusalem, where they will kill me." Peter, speaking as he often did for all of them, was outraged: "Don't even say that!" Jesus doesn't tell his disciples how he will die, but he and his friends must have known. He made the authorities, both civil and religious, profoundly uncomfortable. He was dangerous to the established order of Roman rule. He was being watched; Herod knew who he was and was fascinated but uneasy. Jesus was walking toward his own crucifixion.

Crucifixion was the everyday method of Roman execution, designed to maximize pain, prolong suffering, and deprive the condemned of his last shred of dignity. It provided both public entertainment and a warning to potential malefactors. Crucifixion, the very thought of which fills me with horror, was in the Roman Empire a fairly ordinary method of execution, with Jesus as just one more condemned man, sentenced to an excruciating death.

Unspeakable pain is "excruciating." Cross, or *crux*, is at the heart of the word and the strongest one we have to designate suffering; it is much more powerful than the current practice of asking the patient to choose a number between one and ten. (I've hit a four or a five a few times, but cannot imagine a ten.)

And the cumulative pain of the prolonged ritual of crucifixion must go far beyond ten or twenty or fifty.

Jesus seems to have known this in advance when he set his face toward Jerusalem. He understood how the drama would unfold: first, a vicious scourging of the whip that would leave his shoulders and back lacerated. Then the burden of carrying his cross from Pilate's headquarters to Golgotha. Despite tradition, scholars are not sure exactly where that was, but the walk, even if a few feet, was long enough. Artists have depicted him as dragging the whole cross, which weighed about three hundred pounds, but the condemned man carried only the crossbeam and Simon of Cyrene the rest.

At his trial, he must have been exhausted. After his arrest in the garden, he was passed back and forth all night from the high priests and the counsel, then sent to a reluctant Pilate, who seemed to want no part in his arrest but nevertheless sent him to Herod, who just happened to be in the city. According to legend, Herod entered Jerusalem from a different gate just as Jesus triumphantly came into the city, coming as a king, fulfilling the Hebrew scriptures and mounted on a donkey. Legend or fact, this is powerful drama, sharpening the focus as Jesus' days on earth draw to a close.

Luke tells is that "when Herod saw Jesus, he was very glad, for he had been wanting to see him for a long time, because he had heard about him and was hoping to see him perform some sign" (Luke 23:8). Jesus has become a curiosity. When he refused to play the game and stood mute before Herod, he was roughed up, mocked, and sent back to Pilate.

All this in just a few hours. Was he thirsty? His last drink had probably been the shared cup with his friends at the Passover supper. Had he been able to sit down, even for a few minutes, after his arrest in the garden? Did his captors push him roughly, force him to move quickly even when he was exhausted? Did he see even one neutral face, let alone a friendly one, among those who surrounded him? Had he watched his friends turn their backs and slip away into the night? Now Herod was probably his best bet, but Jesus refused to play the game.

So his walk began. He had promised his friends that after three days, he would rise again as good as new, even better. Did the memory of those words eat at him? Perhaps the whole thing had been one big mistake.

We all know the story. Artists have painted the walk to Golgotha over and over again. Dramas have been written—the most famous of them the Passion Play in Oberammergau, Germany, first performed in 1634 as an expression of gratitude by the inhabitants of that village when the bubonic plague had passed them by. It is still performed every ten years, the little town filling up with the devout and the curious. Long ago, on a walking trip in Bavaria, I stayed overnight in the local inn. The proprietor was a quite pleasant, ordinary-seeming man, but every ten years he got to portray Jesus. I wasn't quite sure how to address him.

Over the centuries, folk piety has added details. Jesus falls three times: this is not only painful but a humiliating sign of weakness. Each time he resumes the walk, he must have been weaker. Did someone help him up or kick him? He meets his mother; it is unbearable to think about that encounter. An unnamed woman wipes the sweat from his face and carries away the imprint of his likeness on the cloth. Her name turns out not to have been Veronica, which in folklore means "true image," but more likely a Miriam or a Sarah, a housewife, a compassionate bystander in the crowd.

The walk ends at Golgotha, the place of the skull, on a hill in the blazing midday sun. But for Jesus' followers, it is just a beginning. Even as they hide out from the authorities, his disciples are probably remembering his words: "If you want to be my friends, take up your cross and walk with me." Luke's gospel adds another significant little word: "Take up your cross *daily* and follow me" (Luke 9:23). Again and again. You might be able to put it down overnight, but pick it up again in the morning.

It took me quite a while—years, actually—to realize that Jesus is not inviting me to be crucified. I'm just volunteering to pick up my cross and carry it. Maybe not with grace or even steadiness, moving ahead under its weight. And it's my cross, not the cross Jesus was compelled to bear, and it may not weigh three hundred pounds. I suspect that in our lifetime we each have a whole assortment of crosses, all distinctly ours. Some are so heavy that we will stagger and fall beneath their weight. Some cut cruelly into our shoulders. Some might be real works of art, skillfully carved from beautifully grained hard wood—the maple cross, the cherry cross, the old oaken cross, the everyday cross, even the invisible cross. Some are so light that they are almost a joke, plywood or plastic, impressive to look at but not to be taken seriously.

To take up my cross at all, let alone *daily*, sounds generous and heroic, especially if it is one of those days when I would rather not. "No time today, but I'll pick it up on Friday. . . It's Sunday, so can't I have a day off? . . . I've got the flu and have to write a sermon—can't I put this off until I feel better?"

But Jesus' command is inexorable: if you want to walk with me, there are no excuses. No days off. You're obsessed with riding your stationary bike every day and taking all your vitamins and checking your e-mail and flossing your teeth. Well, this is your real obligation. It won't kill you. You might get tired or bored or scared or fed up, but this is the condition for your walk with me. It doesn't happen any other way. Put on your sandals or your sneakers or your hefty boots. Pick up that cross and let's get going.

Chapter 17

The Miracle of the Chance Encounter

Now on that same day two of them were going to a village called Emmaus, about seven miles from Jerusalem, and talking with each other about all these things that had happened. While they were talking and discussing, Jesus himself came near and went with them, but their eyes were kept from recognizing him. And he said to them, "What are you discussing with each other while you walk along?" They stood still, looking sad. Then one of them, whose name was Cleopas, answered him, "Are you the only stranger in Jerusalem who does not know the things that have taken place there in these days?" (Luke 24:13–18)

The terrible Friday is past, and now it is three days later, Easter morning. The women have seen the empty tomb and encountered the risen Jesus, but the word hasn't spread to his disciples who are gathered together, frightened and grieving, in Jerusalem. Luke doesn't make clear why Cleopas and his unnamed companion are on their way to the village of Emmaus, seven miles from Jerusalem. Some of Jesus' followers have gathered there, but we aren't told who they are or why they have chosen this village. Are they in hiding from the Romans? Or is this their home town, and there is nowhere else to go? Luke doesn't tell us.

Only Luke tells this story of the companionable walk with the risen but unrecognizable Jesus. It is a powerful story, one that invites me to tag along and eavesdrop. I find great comfort in the fact that—unlike Peter, James, and John, who encountered the transfigured Christ—these two were definitely second-stringers. Cleopas has no previous history, and he and his companion never show up again in the story, which is a pity. If nothing else, their grief and loyalty remind me that the circle around Jesus, the followers who loved him and grieved was much larger than the twelve listed in Scripture and depicted in Leonardo's *Last Supper*.

When I think about them at all, I find myself wishing the two had been accorded even minor saint status, so that we other second-stringers could remember them annually and, more importantly, identify with them as sincere followers of Jesus who are nevertheless slow on the uptake. And welcome them as patrons of all storytellers. For as they walk, they tell and retell the events of the past week: the final meal together, the betrayal of their teacher, his torture and cruel death. Perhaps they reproach themselves because, unlike Mary, those other women disciples, and John, they couldn't bear to stay and watch as he died. And now the latest news—some women have actually visited the tomb and found it empty. And several of them have claimed they encountered Jesus himself risen from the dead, walking and talking!

Walking is conducive to telling stories. What else is there to do? It's hard to read while you are walking along, although I do sometimes encounter people on crowded city streets, engrossed in a book. It strikes me as a little dangerous; with a really absorbing book it's easy to trip on a curb or step into traffic. We need our eyes for walking, especially when the scene is lively. And of course, whether strolling or marching purposefully, people are using their walking time to talk on cell phones, flirt or conduct business, and send text messages. I pity them because they are missing the whole point of walking. Walking alone, you can tell stories to yourself.

Walking with a friend is even better. Of course, old friends can walk in silence just as they can sit side by side for hours without a spoken word between them. This is how I figure out who my real friends are: we don't need a flood of words to draw us together. Pleasant as uninhibited chatter may be, shared silence can be much more intimate. Angry people can walk in silence so that they can pretend that the other is not there, is far away on another path or (preferably) left far behind. But good companions use the time for telling stories. After all, telling stories doesn't kill time: telling stories enriches every moment.

I wonder how many times Cleopas and his companion told the story to each other, perhaps adding details here and there, perhaps falling into silence to reflect, question, and wonder. Perhaps they interrupted each other, adding details, correcting each other's versions, or raising new questions. To tell and retell the story is a common and necessary way of dealing with the shock of loss. Grief must be slow; it calls for patience, for telling and retelling the story in minute detail even when the telling is agony. I recall the heavy hours after the death of my father when my mother almost mechanically repeated the details of his last moments over and over. I was young then and hope that I hid my impatience, but I could see no reason for the endless repetition. Now I know that she had to in order to make it real. She had to imprint each minute detail on her memory, making sure that it would remain with her for the rest of her life. The story was all that she had to hold onto.

Cleopas and his fellow walker had more than their teacher's death on the cross to recall. If what they heard was correct, there was also the mysterious disappearance of his body. Perhaps they also tried to recollect those hopeful times, those times of warmth and friendship, when the way seemed clear, when it seemed as if companionship with their teacher could go on forever, despite his warnings that death awaited him in Jerusalem.

The telling of stories just happens. Of course we tell stories by appointment, as with a spiritual director or a psychotherapist, or (perhaps carefully condensed and edited to save time) to our family doctor. Narrative is at the heart of these relationships, but they are asymmetrical, unequal, and rarely is there give and take. But the true telling of stories does not require an appointment; it's not the same as submitting a report or being interviewed for a job There is mutuality; in telling the story there is give and take, room for silence, room for tears, and room for laughter. Unlike an appointment, an interview, a report, there is no one person sitting behind a desk, listening professionally to the other. We understand the story in its telling as we share it with our listener. It becomes part of us. In good psychotherapy and good spiritual direction, it's all in the telling. It's not the same as a written narrative: there must be a listener.

It's no accident that little kids like stories. They're smart enough to recognize spiritual, indeed human, reality when they meet it. As I recall myself as a child, everything was a story. So I grew up enraptured by stories, willing to hear them again and again without one word being changed. For me, everything is still a story.

And I come by it honestly. If she were alive today, my New England grandmother would be all over the country offering workshops in story-telling with business cards and brochures and probably her own professional web site. She told the same stories endlessly, over and over. The rest of the family politely tuned her out, but I couldn't get enough of her long-ago girlhood on an Illinois farm and the one-room school house where her brother Henry—the mischievous one—once released a couple of squirrels. She made the great Chicago fire of 1871 seem like yesterday, even though she was just a little girl far from the city. As she talked, I could see the night horizon light up and wonder what it was—a divine sign? The end of the world?

She recalled the stories of her pioneer forebears, of her own great-grandmother who sat up all night with a rifle across her knees. The Indians down by the creek had appeared at the cabin door demanding whisky from the family barrel. She sent them on their way, but was uneasy for the rest of the night.

One of my favorites was the account of Great-Great-Uncle Johnny, laid out in his coffin. Apparently the male mourners had dipped too frequently into the barrel on the porch. As time passed, they grew sadder and sadder: no way could they part with Uncle Johnny without some remembrance of him. So they pulled him out of his coffin, propped him up against the rain barrel, and took his picture. (My grandmother never explained where the camera came from.) So Uncle Johnny was very real to me, there in his best and only suit, somehow he managing to look fairly dignified leaning against the rain barrel of a ramshackle farm house.

So my grandmother understood the power of narrative. She understood that stories cannot be hurried, that their words were like footsteps on a long walk. And seven miles is a long walk. Cleopas and his companion probably moved at a steady pace, but there was no need to rush, no point in hurrying. Their destination was in sight, but the journey was going to take time.

What made them trust this stranger who suddenly joined them without explanation? And when he seemed ready to move on, what made them call him back to continue with them on their walk? It was no half-hearted invitation. Luke tells "they urged him strongly, saying 'Stay with us, because it is almost evening and the day is now nearly over.'" We can see this as an act of hospitality: they knew where they were going, they knew that they would soon be with their friends having a shared meal, and they knew that their new companion would be welcome. But I suspect that theirs was much more than a sincere invitation to supper: they yearned for the continued presence of their fellow traveler.

It's almost impossible to imagine life before television, but I grew up addicted to the radio, although not today's intellectually challenging NPR or the vituperative talk shows. Rather the radio dramas of my childhood offered predictable, hackneyed stories that left even the most naive listener feeling superior to the slow-witted characters. It seems almost blasphemous to compare the encounter on the road to Emmaus with weekly episodes of the Lone Ranger. Yet the similarity haunts me: week after week, the mysterious masked man would arrive in some small town just in time to rescue the inhabitants from disaster. Then he would ride away, expecting no thanks or even recognition. As he disappeared, some naive villager would ask, "Who was that masked man?" And the local wise old codger would reply, "Why, sonny, that was the Lone Ranger."

The show went on for years, decades. Even fairly sophisticated adults never tired of the weekly chance encounter with the savior who didn't look the part. Even as a child, I was impatient with their obtuseness. Now, as an adult, I am impatient with my own. If he would stick to the impractical white robe and sandals even in winter, I might be able to pick Jesus out in a crowd. I might still mistake him for the homeless person, almost literally a bundle of rags, who sits on the sidewalk by my subway station. I might mistake him for the taciturn surgeon who once saved my life. I might mistake him for one of our parish teenagers who isn't too grown up to give me a spontaneous hug that almost knocks me over. I might mistake him for the total stranger who offers me the gift of a tiny act of random kindness. I might mistake him for the unacceptable person, the blemish on my carefully maintained landscape. The list goes on and on. And on.

If nothing else, the story of this encounter is a powerful reminder of the sheer ordinariness of miracles. All too often we recognize them only in retrospect.

Perhaps it is more accurate to call this walk to Emmaus a *seemingly* chance encounter. As I look back on my decades, I realize more and more that there are really no accidents, no chance encounters No matter how twisted or straight the road might seem, not matter what unlikely folk might join us for a stretch of a few feet or a few miles, our walk is not a casual wandering. If we see our lives as the long walk between two thresholds, we know that, while it can be lonely, it can never be solitary. Yes, there are good companions like the unnamed disciple who walked with Cleopas. Yes, there are other encounters—some of them dangerous, some annoying, and many of them unexpected. These are chance encounters with the holy, those seemingly random encounters with Jesus, the inveterate walker. He just shows up with no appointment and not dressed as we expect. He refuses to look the part as he walks among us.